D0094048

THE FREE DRINK

THE GAMBLING ADDICTION EPIDEMIC

ADDICTION OF THE MIND

MICHAEL GALLEGOS BORRESEN

ISBN 0-7414-4275-2

Published by:

INFI∞ITY
PUBLISHING.COM

1094 New DeHaven Street, Suite 100
West Conshohocken, PA 19428-2713
Info@buybooksontheweb.com
www.buybooksontheweb.com
Toll-free (877) BUY BOOK
Local Phone (610) 941-9999
Fax (610) 941-9959

Printed in the United States of America

Printed on Recycled Paper

Published January 2008

DEDICATION

This book is dedicated to the millions of addicted compulsive gamblers worldwide who are lost in their life damaging mental addiction. Also for all of those addicted gamblers who have committed suicide, have ended up homeless, went to prison, became in severe financial debt, have gone broke, or who have lost their mental sanity.

FOREWORD

Gambling in the United States and worldwide is very popular and is growing at a very fast rate. Even though gambling can be exciting and fun, the sad part is that the societal acceptance of gambling has given birth to millions of addicted compulsive or pathological gamblers worldwide. This insidious powerful disease addiction of the mind has grown into worldwide epidemic proportions.

Gambling addiction destroys the lives of the addicted gambler as well as their family members. This life destructing addiction is an addiction of the mind that destroys the mental, emotional, and physical health of the addicted gambler. Unfortunately suicide is sometimes the only way out of their misery and many sick gamblers have killed themselves.

The goal of this book is to provide information and to expose this insidious hidden gambling disease as well as breaking apart the whole addictive gambling experience. This book will also help addicted gamblers come to terms with their addiction before they totally destroy their life.

This book is written from an inspirational perspective and from a journalistic perspective as well as from the personal experience of the author, who has been through the whole progressive process of a compulsive gambling addiction. Gambling addiction has become a real pathological disease epidemic that needs to be brought out in the open and be addressed so as to save millions of lives.

CONTENTS

INTRODUCTION

Gambling is very popular in the United States as well as worldwide and is a very lucrative business for those corporations involved in the gambling business. As a result the gambling industry has given birth to millions of sick addicted compulsive or pathological gamblers who are caught up in the fantasy of the gambling addiction disease epidemic worldwide. This disease of the mind has reached epidemic proportions and is growing at a fast rate.

Gambling is accepted as normal behavior by many world governments and is a part of their socioeconomic societies. There is a lot of intentional denial about gambling addiction by governmental politicians and the gambling industry leaders. Addicted gamblers provide the majority of financial revenue for the gambling industry. This powerful addiction to gambling has been hushed for years and has been hidden and kept quiet in the mass media.

The gambling disease is a hidden disease because the illness is an addiction of the mind that is a mental, psychological, and behavioral addiction. Powerful gambling addiction is a clinical disease that is progressive in nature. Gambling addiction can start out as recreational gambling and then turn into problem gambling and then to compulsive gambling and finally into a full blown pathological disorder.

This gambling disease can also be influenced genetically regarding an addicted gambler's personality, temperament, behaviors, and sociability. Many addicted gamblers can be dressed in nice clothes and be well groomed but can be a very sick person within their mind. A powerful gambling addiction is a thinking man's disease and many intellectual thinkers succumb to a gambling addiction.

The disease can be arrested but is not totally curable. An addicted gambler with the gambling disease cannot gamble anymore or else they will continue in a path of self-destructive behavior. Many people can gamble in moderation and not become addicted. This book is about gambling addiction and the different manifestations of this progressive disease. Also included in the book are various observations about the gambling industry and the gambling world.

Las Vegas, Nevada, Atlantic City, and now Macau, China are the top three most popular areas for gamblers who want to spend their hard earned money gambling in the mega casinos or in the smaller casinos or corner bars. Macau, China is going to be bigger than Las Vegas and millions of Chinese citizens are becoming gambling addicts.

Gambling is everywhere. In Las Vegas there are even gambling machines in the corner grocery stores and in laundries. Today gambling can also be found on the internet, Indian reservations, riverboats, cruise ships, churches, and the stock exchanges. Many countries worldwide have some form of a gambling industry.

Gambling is also sensationalized on primetime television shows with the many celebrity poker craze tournaments, which are portrayed as a sport and is drawing in a younger audience into the gambling world. There are also gambling game shows where the contestants are making gambling deals to win thousands of dollars or possibly a million dollars. These gambling shows on television are also showing kids that gambling is normal behavior in the United States and also worldwide.

Today there is some type of gambling in probably every state in the United States with the expansion of casinos being built on Indian reservations. Gambling is a multi-billion dollar created industry that was designed to take your hard earned money. Even churches are involved in gambling with their bingo nights and raffles. Besides the corporations who are in control of the gambling industry, our local, state, and federal governments are involved with gambling.

Gambling for many people starts out by playing a gambling machine or a table game just for fun. The fun can turn into more than just fun and turn into a powerful mental gambling addiction. Some people will get addicted while others can gamble in moderation and not become compulsive gamblers.

My mind got addicted to gambling and I am a gambler that cannot play in moderation. As a result, my life took a detour through the various stages of a compulsive gambling addiction cycle. Today I have snapped out of my powerful addiction and am back on the right path toward living a normal life as a recovering gambler and I have stopped gambling.

This book is written from my personal experience with my gambling addiction and also my observations and knowledge about the various aspects of the gambling world and its environment. This book is also written in an easy to read format so that active gamblers, non-gamblers, and their friends and families can be able to understand better about gambling addiction and the consequences of this insidious addiction of the mind.

My personal hope is for addicted gamblers to wake up from their addiction before their life is totally destroyed. Many addicted gamblers have lost their families, homes, jobs, and have ended up homeless. Many will hit bottom and at the lowest point of their misery and depression will commit suicide. Others will become in debt for life and spend the rest of their life restoring themselves back to some form of financial health. The fortunate gamblers who snap out of their gambling addiction will spend the rest of their lives recovering from their addiction and being restored to mental health and start living and enjoying life.

I titled the book, "The Free Drink" because the free drink is the trick or gimmick that is used to lure people into gambling. Many gamblers will spend hundreds of dollars gambling and will give the cocktail waitress or bartender a good monetary tip. The gambler will go home and suffer from gamblers remorse once they realize how much money that they threw away gambling. They did get "free" drinks.

People in general do not realize the significance of the free drink in direct relationship to the effect it has on compulsive gambling addiction. The "free drink" is portrayed to the general public as a generous offer that is given to gamblers by cocktail waitresses dressed in sexy costumes.

These free drinks can also be addicting because of the alcohol and the mind-altering experience that takes place when combined with fantasy gambling. The underlying job function of the cocktail waitress is to give alcohol to the gambling customers so that they will spend more money and spend more time gambling in their respective gambling establishment.

My personal gambling addiction affected every area of my life. My recovery from my compulsive gambling addiction is ongoing and I will never graduate from this powerful life damaging addiction. As my recovery improves so does my personal life.

The main goal in recovery is to restore the mind back to a normal way of thinking from the abnormal way of thinking that was caused up by the constant gambling. At the present time I am living and enjoying life instead of existing as a brainwashed zombie behind a gambling machine.

Most of my observations regarding the gambling addiction epidemic are from my experiences in Las Vegas, Nevada. The gambling environment of Las Vegas is very similar to other gambling resorts. Las Vegas has been the gambling capital for several years. Today gambling resorts are increasing all over the world.

This book is about gambling addiction and about the gambling industry that promotes gambling addiction and not about trashing the various gambling resorts like Las Vegas. Cities like Las Vegas are fun to visit if you are not a compulsive addicted gambler.

Today I am a freelance journalist living in Las Vegas, Nevada. I have lived in Las Vegas for 13 years and I have lived in the gambling world as an active addicted gambler and as a recovering gambling addict. My goal in writing this book is to provide some sunshine on the dark world of the gambling addiction epidemic.

1

THE GAMBLING INDUSTRY

The gambling industry is about a $400 billion dollar per year business just in the United States. The worldwide amount is astronomical and is growing. More money is spent on legal gambling than is spent on other recreational events combined. This includes movies, sports, video games, recorded music, or theme parks.

Many groups are involved in the gambling industry from governments, politicians, corporations, Indian reservations, and possibly still white collar entrepreneurs. The economics of the gambling industry is supported by the millions of gamblers with a compulsive gambling addiction or who have progressed into a psychiatric pathological gambling addiction.

Gambling in the United States is growing at an alarming fast rate. In the United States people can gamble legally at approximately 1,000 casinos. About 500 Las Vegas type casinos operate in 11 states and 500 casinos are on American Indian reservations in 29 states. Today people can even stay at home and gamble on the internet with their credit cards regardless if they are of legal age.

The legalization of gambling has been widely supported and accepted by city, state, and the federal government. Money talks in a capitalist society. The various governments benefit from the gambling industry with tax collections, job creation, and regional economic development. Politicians will usually receive large campaign donations from the executives in the gambling industry.

Gambling in the United States used to be organized and ran by organized crime families and today is organized and ran by professional corporations. When the corporations took over the gambling industry, they changed the name of their industry from gambling to gaming. The gambling industry corporations were also placed on the stock market. Over the years gambling has come from suppression to acceptance.

There are governmental commissions that oversee legalized gambling within their jurisdiction. Gambling has become so popular that many states have government sponsored lotteries. The reasoning for the lotteries is that the money donated is used for special purposes like education. Gambling creates a lot of jobs at the expense of the addicted gambler.

Since 1989, casino-style gambling has spread across the United States on American Indian reservations. About 11 states have Indian casinos and almost every Indian reservation have smaller gambling halls. Some of the states that have casino-style casinos are California, New Mexico, Nevada, Colorado, Oklahoma, Louisiana, Florida, Minnesota, Wisconsin, North Dakota, South Dakota, and Oregon. Oklahoma has the greatest number of casinos per capita.

Many gambling industry leaders believe that gambling has positive social values, maintaining that gambling provides a form of adult play. Also that gambling provides enjoyment to elderly citizens and others who otherwise would have no entertainment outlet.

This expensive adult play has created millions of addicted compulsive gamblers, including senior citizens with fixed incomes. In Las Vegas many casinos send shuttle buses to pick up senior citizens so that they can act out their compulsive gambling behavior at their gambling establishment.

The gambling industry in Las Vegas also includes corner bars, grocery stores, drug stores, and self-service laundries. There are also small gambling outlets in shopping malls. Gambling is in every neighborhood in Las Vegas.

The corner bar is very popular among locals in Las Vegas and the most popular game of choice is video poker. The various games of video poker are the most addicting gambling games. It is said that addiction to video poker is like being addicted to crack and cocaine. The corner bar is also sort of a cult environment with several regular brainwashed compulsive gamblers religiously gambling their money away.

People in Las Vegas can go to a grocery store just to buy a loaf of bread and easily spend $200 dollars in a video poker or slot machine. The gambling machines are conveniently located at the exits of the grocery stores. It is not just the major grocery stores but also the quick stop convenience stores that have gambling twenty-four hours a day.

Gambling is also at the McCarran International Airport in Las Vegas. When airline passengers first step into any terminal at the airport, they are greeted by several gambling machines. The sound of the machines as well as the visual of the various slot machines is a tease and an introduction into the Las Vegas gambling environment.

In our present day society in the United States, gambling is everywhere and has become accepted as merely a form of recreation. The gambling industry will continue to grow because it is a very lucrative and profitable industry. Since gambling is open 24 hours and everyday, there is a steady constant cash flow into the corporations and their respective gambling enterprises.

The financial revenue that allows the gambling industry to become profitable is donated by addicted gamblers whom are habitual losers and not winners. Various gambling casinos and other gambling businesses also become profitable by being on the stock market. The billions of dollars profited by the gambling industry worldwide goes to the corporation executives. The billions of dollars also goes to building bigger mega casinos and causing the gambling industry to continue to grow bigger and bigger.

2

THE GAMBLING GAME

Gambling is probably the biggest created monetary game that has taken the hard earned money of many people worldwide for several years. The success of the gambling game is that it is well accepted by those leaders in our governments and is portrayed in our society as a normal way of behavior. Children are raised up with the false belief that gambling is merely a part of life. The gambling game is portrayed with a pretty face but there is a dark ugly face to gambling. The gambling game is well thought out and orchestrated so as to fool the general public into donating their money into the gambling industry.

The Las Vegas Strip is very pretty at night with all the neon lights lighting up the mega casinos. The Strip at night transforms into an adult Disney Land full of fantasy and illusion. About 50 million tourists travel to Las Vegas per year and the majority of them are fantasy gamblers dreaming of winning a big jackpot of money. The general public will get lost in the Las Vegas Strip created illusion and fantasy and not realize that this fantasy was built in the middle of a desert.

All the mega casinos in Las Vegas, Atlantic City, or Macau, China or some other gambling resort were built by gambling losers and not gambling winners. Compulsive gamblers pay the light bills for the mega casinos on the Strip at night. The gambling industry would not function if there were not addicted gamblers throwing their money away.

The main part of the gambling game is to create an environment of fantasy temptation that will play upon the fantasies of the minds of potential gamblers and seduce them into donating their money. The sad thing is that the fantasy is promoted to many people who already have some form of mental issue or condition.

Many of these mental disorders like schizophrenia or bipolar have people living in a rich fantasy world already. Others will have an obsessive compulsive disorder that makes them set up to become compulsive or pathological gamblers. They will fit right in and feel good when the gambling fantasy gets into their already diseased minds. The created fantasy that the gambling industry creates and promotes is also a mental escape for people who want to get away from the realties of life and their personal problems.

The majority of sick compulsive gamblers or pathological gamblers are lonely introverts. The fantasy of gambling becomes their best friend and they will live in a dream world for several months or years. These people are taken advantage of by the casinos by taking their money with no concern for their physical or mental health. The casinos will cater to these addicted gamblers as long as they are donating money.

Another goal of the gambling game is to make potential gamblers feel accepted and at home within their gambling establishment. The addicted gambler will be given false conditional love by the casino hosts and the cocktail waitresses or bartenders. The same method is used that religious cults use in bonding with their recruits. A lonely gambler can find some type of false family in a casino or a gambling bar. This fake acceptance and love can be very addicting in combination with the gambling.

There are several tricks and gimmicks created by the gambling industry managements, whether it is a huge mega casino or a corner bar. The purpose is to recruit and seduce people into becoming gamblers and hopefully addicted gamblers who will spend a lot of time and money in their respective gambling business. A lot of these tricks, gimmicks, or promotions are created by professional commercial psychologists or professional marketing and advertising people. Their goal is to manipulate the minds and emotions of the general public.

The free drink is the most widely used gimmick that lures people to gamble and keeps the active gamblers gambling. A sexy friendly female cocktail waitress dressed in a revealing sexy costume walks around the gamblers playing the slot machines or table games and serves them free drinks. The perception is that you are getting free drinks but in reality those free drinks could cost you a hundred dollars to a lifetime of compulsive gambling. The more alcohol that a gambler intakes into their brain chemistry will cause them to lose their common sense and will they enter into the fantasy world of gambling. The alcohol will alter the brain chemistry and as a result will change the perception of reality to a perception of fantasy.

Another widely use gimmick besides the free drink is the inexpensive food. Drinks and food appeal to the physical needs of the gambling patrons. These meal bargains bring people into the gambling establishment. Every casino has an all you can eat buffet or a 24-hour coffee shop with good food bargains. There are several gambling machines close to the buffet where a person with a full stomach can sit and gamble while their food settles. The all you can eat buffets can also be very addicting.

Another gimmick that is used is that regular compulsive gamblers will be given free meals so as to keep them happy and keep them coming back. The gambler could have spent a thousand dollars gambling and is then awarded a free meal or buffet for his or her hard work gambling. This also makes the regular compulsive gambler feel somewhat good because they feel that they are receiving special attention.

Sex is also used as a gimmick to draw people into a casino and to lure potential gamblers. From the topless revue shows to the sexy scantily dressed cocktail waitresses, sex is very appealing to the fantasy world of the addicted gambler. Gambling environments have a lot of eye candy walking around.

Prostitution is illegal in Las Vegas but is over-looked and tolerated by casino management and local law enforcement. Many casinos have in house call girls that are provided to their gamblers who are high rollers that donate a lot of money to the casino. The sex trade attracts a lot of gamblers to gamble in the casinos as sex becomes part of the gambling fantasy world.

Independent hookers can be seen around the casino bars trying to solicit potential foolish men to go to a hotel room and provide their services for a price. These hookers are tolerated by casino management because they draw men with money into their gambling establishment.

The dealing of cards is a very simple endeavor. Then why do card dealers have to go to a dealer's school for two to three months or even longer in order to deal blackjack or poker games. The casinos only hire dealers who have graduated from one of these dealer's schools. These schools are very secretive and are a closed society.

In the card dealing schools the students are taught how to manipulate a card deck so that the winning hands are in the casino's favor. They learn how to deal cards from the top or bottom of the deck or even how to deal the second card from the top. This will give the card dealer a winning hand or change the rotation of the card deck. Some advanced card dealer students will learn the advance skill of counting cards.

Any gambler who is caught counting cards or manipulating a card game will be kicked out of the casino by security and will be considered a criminal. Many of the criminal card manipulators are former casino card dealers who went from legal card manipulating to illegal card manipulating.

The purpose of these dealing schools is to teach card dealers how to perform tricky card manipulation in order to bring in revenue for the casino. They also learn about the rules of the gambling industry regarding the intake of the cash flow. The dealers or other casino workers are supposed to encourage the gamblers to gamble and donate their money. A dealer or casino worker could get fired it they tell a compulsive gambler to take a break or merely to go and get a cup of coffee.

Another gimmick is to have various promotions like spinning a wheel for cash if a gambler cashes their paycheck at the casino. Once the gambler has cashed their paycheck and has money in their hands, then it is hard not to resist the temptation to gamble. Many times a gambler will plan on spending only twenty dollars but end up wasting away their whole paycheck.

In order to keep track of gamblers that visit a casino, the casinos issue out players cards with the gambler's name on the card. These cards look like a prestigious credit card and they make a person feel like if they are a member of a prestigious association, which happens to be the casino. In order to get a card the gambler must provide an official governmental identification. Their personal information is entered into a central database that records the amount of time that the gambler spends gambling in their gambling establishment. As a gambler plays they accumulate player's points that can be redeemed for various award prizes.

The gimmick with these player's cards is that a gambler will be awarded prizes like a free buffet or a free room. This depends on the number of player's points that is accumulated on their card. The word free is always used in this player card gimmick. In reality a gambler could have spent hundreds or thousands of dollars gambling but since they have accumulated a lot of player's points, then they will receive a free prize award.

Casinos are like banks and will lend some gamblers money on casino credit. This is called markers in the gambling world. The problem is that the money has to be paid back like any other personal loan. Many gamblers will become in debt to a casino after losing the casino money that they borrowed. The casino will then have control over a gambler's life until the money is paid back. Many compulsive gamblers have had to sell their houses or other assets in order to pay back the casino bank.

Many casinos in Las Vegas and other places will send a courtesy shuttle bus to a senior citizen retirement home or apartment complex to pick up senior citizens and bring them to their gambling establishment. It is portrayed as a goodwill gesture by providing some entertainment for our older citizens by allowing them to play bingo, slots, table games, or other gambling games.

Many of these senior citizens will become addicted compulsive gamblers and give their money to the casino. The sad part is that many of these senior citizens are on fixed incomes and are throwing their money away. There are several horror stories about senior citizens losing their hard earned retirement pension to their gambling addiction.

The mass media and the advertising community help gambling establishments promote their money making operation. This promotion by the mass media makes gambling to appear as normal behavior and that gambling is just a part of everyday living and a way of life.

There are always stories on the local news about gamblers who win big jackpots or stories that are in favor of the gambling industry. The mass media will usually only show positive stories about the gambling world and not the negative stories. The goal is to please the gambling industry businesses who make up a lot the advertising money that supports television or print media.

The role of the news media whether it be television or newspapers is to promote the gambling and not to show human interest stories regarding the compulsive gamblers who are caught up in the gambling addiction epidemic. A human interest story that is directly related to gambling addiction is the high rate of bankruptcies and home foreclosures.

The casino advertisers utilize professional commercial advertisers and psychologists to assist with the creation of seductive advertisements that will draw in potential gamblers. These advertisements are usually designed to appeal to the fantasies of the general public. Fantasy and illusion are gimmicks used to lure in people to casinos and gambling.

People in Las Vegas and other cities are committing suicide while some will end up in a general or mental hospital or end up in jail. There are about 400 suicides in Las Vegas per year and Nevada is the second highest state for suicide rates in the United States. Car accidents, homicide, domestic assault, robberies, burglaries, or other accidents or criminal activities are related to gambling addiction.

These negative stories are kept hushed by the news media. They never make the front page news and if they do the relation to gambling addiction is never mentioned. Many sick depressed gamblers jump to their deaths from their casino hotel room or from a parking garage. Others will overdose on alcohol or drugs after a bad gambling day.

The mass media and the advertisement community play a huge role in luring people into the gambling environment and some of these people will become addicted compulsive gamblers. At the same time the negative stories related to gambling addiction are kept quiet by the mass media. They are all part of the larger gambling game. The casinos or other gambling establishments have the money to pay for slick seductive advertisements, which are aired on television or printed in the print media.

The gambling game is a well thought out and created game. Their goal is to get people to gamble and donate their money to their money making business establishment. They have been very successful and have given birth to millions of addicted compulsive gamblers. Another important fact about the gambling game is that gambling is supported by politicians and others in leadership within our local, state, and federal governments.

In the past when the organized crime mob was in charge of the gambling industry they were always suspicious and especially in Las Vegas. Government law enforcement would keep tabs on the mob's casinos. The FBI would sometimes raid or pay a visit to a casino to observe their operation or to review their financial books and records. Back then gambling was not so well accepted by the government and society in general.

There was a transformation when huge corporations saw the large amounts of money that comes from a created gambling business operation and they soon took over the gambling industry from the mob. Soon the gambling industry was placed on the stock market and the industry took off with the construction of the mega casinos. Today the gambling industry is well accepted by our government and within our society and is perceived as pure recreation. Gambling has become well accepted worldwide as normal behavior and a way of life.

In order for gambling to be legal within the various gambling establishments, the casinos or other gambling businesses need to get a government issued gambling license. When the corporations took control of the gambling change they did something very slick and changed the word gambling to gaming. Their goal is to brainwash the public with the word gaming and not use the word gambling.

The gambling industry then became regulated by politicians within our state and federal governments.

Politicians who were on the campaign trail would get a financial donation from the leaders of the various casinos or other gambling businesses if they support their view on gambling and are in favor of the gambling industry endeavors.

In Nevada there is an organization called the Nevada Council On Problem Gambling. There primary goal is to try to help problem gamblers get help for their gambling addiction. They have created a brochure that gives a hotline number for addicted gamblers to call for help. In order for casinos and other gambling businesses to operate they must have copies of this brochure posted and made available to gamblers. This gives the perception that the casino or other gambling operation are concerned about problem gambling.

These brochures are placed in places that are not too visible for gamblers to notice. A good example is that they are placed on the side of an ATM machine instead of the front. The problem or compulsive gambler goes to the ATM to get money to feed their addiction and not to pick up a brochure that is on the side of the ATM machine.

On the front cover of the brochure are the words, "WHEN THE FUN STOPS." When the fun stops could mean anything and the word gambling or problem is not on the front cover. There is also a picture of a setting sun on the ocean horizon. A person's eye is drawn to the beautiful view of the setting sun. Inside the brochure is information about problem gambling. In order to read the brochure inside a gambler must get past the illusion of the setting sun on the ocean. For a compulsive or pathological gambler, they will continue to gamble uncontrollably even when the fun stops.

Younger generations are getting hooked to gambling at a young age. Kids are growing up with the belief that gambling is normal and just part of life. Casinos want to get our children addicted by placing gambling games in a smaller scale in their game arcades. Casino arcades are like mini casinos for children. When the children turn twenty one then they will move onto the main casino floor and gamble their money away. Children are also watching gambling on television and on the internet. The goal is to produce addicted gamblers at a young age.

The American Medical Association reported that about five million children are addicted to video games. This addiction to video games is also a visual addiction of the mind in the same manner that compulsive gambling is. The American Medical Association report also calls addictive behavior to video games a psychiatric disorder. The majority of slot machines created for gambling today also happen to be interactive entertaining video games.

The movie theaters in Las Vegas are located and attached to a casino. In order to go and see a movie; adults, adolescents, or children need to go to a casino. Many will walk through the inside of the casino and pass by the many gambling machines or table games. This is a prearranged agreement with the various movie theaters so as to get people into their casino. Gambling images gets instilled into minds of the younger generation and the gambling seeds are planted.

Those in leadership of the gambling industry or the gaming industry know exactly what they are doing. A majority of the leaders or the workers within the gambling industry do not gamble themselves. The sad part is that the general public can be easily fooled and get caught up in the gambling fantasy and can be easily tricked out of their hard earned money.

Those who are participants in the greater gambling game whether it be in Las Vegas, Atlantic City, Macau, China, a Indian reservation, or the corner bar are only concerned with the revenue monetary profits that they get from sick compulsive addicted gamblers. There is not much concern if these compulsive or pathological gamblers cause self-destruction to themselves or their families.

3

GAMBLING ENVIRONMENT

The gambling environment is a created seductive environment that is created to appeal to the senses and emotions of the visiting customers and potential gamblers. The majority of gambling environments also appeal to the fantasy side of the brain.

Many people who do not want to deal with reality will choose to escape into a fantasy gambling environment. They stand the risk of possibly becoming gambling addicts and then they start to live in the fantasy world of a casino. The environment of the Las Vegas Strip is one huge fantasyland and adult playground.

The various different categories of gambling environments are the casino, the corner bar, and other places like cruise ships, river boats, grocery stores, laundries, and on the internet. These different places have different set ups but are still designed to lure people in and hopefully take their hard earned money.

The many casinos are designed with a fantasy theme. Casino executives employ commercial psychologists to help with the psychological design of their fantasy world. Casinos form a Disney Land for adults.

The interior environment of casinos are well planned out. Las Vegas is a desert and the casinos cumulatively are a created illusion. The casino is a nice fun place to hang out and one way to spend a lot of time in a casino is to become a gambler. First of all, the casino has a very pretty interior with huge chandeliers and other expensive paintings and artifacts. Escaping to a casino is like escaping into a castle. Many people feel comfortable in casino and a casino could easily become a second home, especially if they are an addicted gambler.

The interior of a casino is a very confusing place and they are designed to be confusing. They want visitors only to focus on gambling. Inside a casino the ceilings are low so that the potential gambler will have eye level contact with the gambling machines or table games. There are no clocks or windows so that a person could lose their sense of time while they are gambling. The carpet on the floors is very confusing and is hard to focus on. The focus again is on gambling. Casinos are also designed as a maze so that a gambler will lose their sense of direction.

Casinos are like gambling cults with their own personal security. There are surveillance cameras everywhere inside and outside the casino. The casinos are also private property and they can do whatever they want to with their bad customers. The bad customers are the ones who are perceived as cheating. Casinos have small secret rooms where they can take bad customers until the police come to pick them up or they can also emotionally or physically harass the bad customer. Other people who are seen as loiterers who are not spending money in the casino will usually be kicked out.

The cocktail waitresses are pretty females and are dressed sexy with skimpy uniforms that show off their body curves. Many of the cocktail waitresses also wear push up bras to extenuate their upper body. They are nice to look at. Many gamblers will spend hours in a casino to look at the cocktail waitresses and order free drinks from them. Only active gamblers will receive free drinks from the sexy cocktail waitresses.

The action of the casino environment is also very exciting. There is a lot of noise with the combination of the gambling machines and people talking and laughing. There is also very good music in the background. A band performs in the casino lounges that are close to the gambling games.

The local corner bar is also very popular amongst gamblers. Many people prefer a smaller gambling environment other than the big fancy mega casino environment. In Las Vegas there are corner bars on almost every block and they have several gambling machines. The main gambling machine is video poker. Many locals get hooked on the video poker machines and are compulsive gamblers. Addiction to video poker is like being addicted to crack cocaine.

The corner bars are also decorated inside to make people feel comfortable and stay awhile and always come back. The corner bar staff are very friendly and they form a superficial bond with their regular customers. Those who work in a gambling environment receive most of their tips from the addicted gamblers. There are also food specials aimed at bringing people in to eat and hopefully to gamble. The active gamblers also receive free drinks just like in a casino.

Other gambling environments are the grocery stores, convenience stores, liquor stores, and self-service laundries. A lot of people take a short trip to their local grocery store to buy milk and bread and end up spending the afternoon gambling and will spend a hundred dollars for milk and bread. Also a quick trip to a convenience store or a liquor store can turn into a long and expensive trip. A person can also go to wash their clothes in a laundry and gamble while there are being washed and also spend a lot of money but they left with clean clothes.

Gambling environments are everywhere world-wide. This is why we have millions of gambling addicts. These gambling environments are very seductive and are definitely fantasy worlds. A person who is lonely and does not want to deal with their real life problems can easily escape into a gambling fantasy environment.

The end result is that the gambling environ-ments are also very addicting in combination with the gambling machines. Also addicting is the superficial special attention that is given to compulsive gamblers by the casino or bar staff. A gambling environment is a fun place to escape to instead of being lonely in a small apartment or house.

— 4 —

FANTASY GAMBLING GAMES

Gambling fantasy games can be divided into different categories. The major categories are video poker machines, interactive video game slots, table games, and community games like bingo and keno. Many addicted gamblers will only focus on one of these game categories while others will compulsively play them all. The fantasy of hitting a jackpot and winning a lot of money by simply playing a game makes these fantasy games very addicting. The fantasy of gambling is definitely part of the addiction of the mind.

Probably the most addictive gambling game is the video poker machine. There is a comparison that the addiction to video poker is as strong as being addicted to crack or cocaine. Video poker machines are everywhere and are very easily available. More and more bars are installing video poker machines as soon as gambling becomes legal in their local community.

Video poker is very entertaining and seductive and there is the fantasy of winning a jackpot with a single hand. Most of the time it takes hundreds of dealt hands to win some money. Everyone is chasing the royal flush, which will pay one thousand dollars with five quarters played or four thousand dollars if five dollars is played per hand. The hands that are dealt by a video poker machine will tease a gambler giving them poker hands that are close to a winning hand.

Addicted video poker players will spend hours and hours trying to get a winning hand. If they lose money then they will return and try to win back their losses. This is called chasing your money and can become a never-ending merry-go-round of insanity. It is said that doing the same thing over and over again and expecting different results is insane behavior. Combine the playing of highly addictive video poker machines with alcohol from the free drinks and a compulsive gambler can spend several hours lost in the fantasy world of video poker.

The various slot machines are very high tech and are addictive video games that are very entertaining. The video slots are interactive and will get into a gambler's psyche. These computerized slot machines are connected to a main computer and many fantasy gamblers do not realize that they are playing against a very sophisticated programmed computer.

There are a lot of penny machines that are very deceiving. A person has to play hundreds of pennies in order to win something. Gamblers could spend five dollars per try but in their mind they are merely playing a penny machine. These penny slot machines can take in money fast and a gambler can go broke playing a penny slot machine.

The most popular table games are blackjack, roulette, and craps. These are social games and a gambler can get addicted to the game as well as to the social atmosphere with the other gamblers. With the free drinks there is a party atmosphere. This can turn into one expensive party and the casino gets the profits.

Today, there is a big poker craze with the many poker tournaments. The players can play for jackpots that can range into the thousands up to a million. The people that play in the poker rooms need to have a lot of money to play with. Addiction to playing poker is not so much about the money, but it is the psychological addiction about outsmarting and manipulating the other human beings playing in your immediate poker game. Compulsive gamblers addicted to playing poker will spend hours and hours in a poker room and the poker room becomes their second and sometimes first home.

There are fantasy gambling games out there for everyone. The games are fun and entertaining and can become very addictive. The games appear with a pretty face but they can also turn ugly when they take your hard earned money. The games will cause a gambler to start chasing their losses and get on the insanity merry-go-round.

A lot of compulsive gamblers will get involved in sports betting, which is also a fantasy game and can be very addicting. They will spend hours at a casino sports betting book betting on horse or dog races as well as major sports like baseball, football, or basketball. Those who place bets at a sports book also are given free drinks that will alter their brain chemistry. As a result they will place several bets and spend a long period of time in the sports book. The sports books can also become a second or first home for many addicted compulsive gamblers.

Lotteries are very big across the United States. Millions of people try their chance at winning a big jackpot by buying several lottery tickets and then fantasizing about what they would do with the millions of dollars they would win when they win the lottery. Many lotteries are being sponsored by state governments and the money is claimed to be used for education purposes. The kids are certainly getting a education that playing lotteries and gambling in general is okay.

Bingo is another popular gambling game. Addicted gamblers will also spend hours and hours in a bingo room with the fantasy of winning a lot of money. Many senior citizens get addicted to playing bingo and they look forward for the casino shuttle bus to pick them up so that they can spend their day gambling. Bingo is also on primetime television today as a game show format. Many churches will also have bingo nights to raise money for their church fund. Churches will also hold raffles. Gambling is everywhere and even in our churches.

Casinos in Las Vegas as well as in other cities and Indian reservations have game arcades for children, adolescents, and adults. These arcades are like mini-casinos for kids. There are several fantasy gambling games in the arcades and will plant the gambling seed and thus begin the brainwashing of our children into the thrill of gambling.

When the kids turn twenty-one then they will be set mentally as compulsive gamblers and will start gambling their money on the main casino gambling floors. You do not see the casino security guards in the game arcades checking the identification of the kids to see if they are old enough to gamble.

The goal of the leaders of the gambling industry is to set up our kids into the fantasy world of gambling at a young age. The fantasy gambling games are provided everywhere worldwide in order to get the world's population addicted to gambling regardless of age or social status.

__ 5 __

MORE THAN JUST FUN

The majority of people start gambling just for fun. They will play a little money here and there so that they can get a free drink. Eventually they will win some jackpot money and make friends with the cocktail waitress or the bartender. They will gamble more and more and then their gambling becomes a recreational hobby. Later on their gambling becomes more than just fun and becomes a bad habit and then a powerful addiction of the mind.

About 50 million tourists travel to Las Vegas to have a fun filled vacation and a majority of them are gamblers. Some of them can gamble in moderation while others are compulsive gamblers. Many of the compulsive gamblers are return visitors to Las Vegas or another gambling mecca. Compulsive gamblers can also gamble on the internet in the privacy of their home. Since gambling is everywhere, a gambler can have "fun" almost anywhere today.

There is a period when the fun stops and a person will become controlled by their obsession and compulsion to gamble. Gambling becomes more than fun and becomes an everyday activity for the addicted gambler. This is when gambling being very seductive and cunning will sneak into the mind, soul, and spirit of a gambler and control their whole being. The gambler is led to believe by the gambling disease that they are just having fun but in reality their gambling addiction is not fun anymore.

Gambling can be a lot of fun when it is done in moderation. Usually the moderation stops and becomes problem gambling and then progresses to compulsive gambling and then possibly pathological gambling. People who already have an addictive personality cannot just gamble for fun. They are already set up for a gambling addiction.

The owners of gambling establishments will advertise in the visual and print media about the fun that a person can have gambling. They use having fun as a means of bringing in potential gamblers into their gambling business.

Casinos have a lot of fun gimmicks and tricks to lure and seduce gamblers. They make it seem that the only place to have fun is in their casino. There is a lot of competition between the various casinos for the money that is being donated by compulsive gamblers.

Gambling can be fun at first but as the gambling addiction disease progresses then the fun will certainly stop. The fun turns into gambler disgust and gambler remorse. Sometimes the gambler will experience incomprehensible demoralization. This is when gambling is no longer fun recreation.

Those people involved in the greater gambling game and in the gambling industry try hard to give the perception that gambling is just fun. For example, the poker craze tournaments are promoted as a fun sporting event. The majority of poker players start out playing just for fun and end up playing poker compulsively and uncontrollably.

Gambling is also promoted by the mass media as pure recreation. Gambling is promoted by the advertising community to be glamorous and merely fun entertainment. We never hear from the media human-interest stories or situations about when gambling is more than fun and becomes an insidious addiction disease.

The dark side of compulsive addiction is kept hushed and out of the public eye. The reason for this is that a majority of the media advertisers come directly from the casino and the larger gambling industry.

It is not fun when an addicted gambler hurts someone else or hurts themselves and possibly commits suicide. It is not fun when and addicted gambler get into severe financial debt. It is not fun when an addicted gambler gets separated from their family. It is not fun when an addicted gambler ends up in prison. It is not fun when an addicted gambler loses their mental sanity.

— 6 —

MIND ADDICTION

A gambling addiction is one of the most powerful addictions to stop because it is an addiction of the mind. Because gambling addiction is mental and psychological, this ugly addiction takes control of almost every part of someone's human experience.

Gambling addiction gets ingrained within a gambler's intellect, cognitive processes, emotions, and their spirit. Gambling addiction just like video game addiction is also a visual addiction, which allows the addictive images to enter the functions of the brain. The information enters the brain through the eyes from the interactive slot machines, computer monitors, or the table games. The brain gets addicted to the processing of the information that is provided by gambling games.

After hours and hours of gambling the brain can get brainwashed and the addicted gambler will enter into a mental state as a hypnotized zombie. When the brain chemistry is altered by the alcohol that is freely given to gamblers, then the brain will definitely go through a transformation into a fantasy state of mind.

This powerful mind addiction is also a behavioral addiction because our behaviors are directly related to our thought processes, which undergo a significant change by many hours, day, months, or years of habitual gambling. We act out what we think. For compulsive or pathological gamblers the gambling disease will do the thinking for them. The addicted gambler will lose control of their rational sane thinking and their addiction to gambling will take over their mind. In other words, a gambling addiction is crazy making. Millions of addicted gamblers who have lost some degree of their healthy mental sanity are supporting the gambling industry. A healthy sane person will not gamble and throw their hard earned money away.

Gambling can also be combined with an alcohol or smoking addiction. Sex addiction can also be involved with the physical attraction of the sexy cocktail waitresses. The total combination of the various addictions in combination with gambling can integrate into someone's total human experience and turn them into a self-destructing addictive person.

The powerfulness of a compulsive gambling addiction will take control of a person and totally change their personality. They will become a different person and they will start not having healthy sane reality thinking but instead start thinking and living in a fantasy world. As a result the addictive gambler will have thinking and living problems and have psychiatric and emotional disorders.

The mind of an addicted gambler will also be brainwashed and controlled by their gambling disease. This is the same way that a person gets addicted to a religious cult and they get brainwashed and they undergo a personality change. By the brainwashing process the belief system changes to the belief system of the religious cult or the gambling industry.

A gambling addiction being a mental, emotional, and a behavioral addiction is harder to break free from than a substance abuse addiction like alcohol or nicotine. In order to break free from a powerful gambling addiction, the addict has to come to a realization that their gambling behavior is self-destructive in nature and is not normal behavior as it appears to be. There is a strong wall of psychological denial that has to be broken through for an addicted gambler to mentally snap out of their addiction and then seek help to recover from this insidious life damaging disease.

Withdrawal from a powerful gambling addiction is a very hard process. There is a lot of psychological and emotional pain that is experienced by the gambler in recovery in order to get healthy again. The cognitive processes, emotions, and behaviors have to be returned so some form of normalcy. A gambling addiction will cause cognitive distortion, which means that the thinking processes of an addicted gambler gets distorted or messed up.

A compulsive or pathological gambler will always be a gambling addict. The gambling addiction disease can go into remission but not be totally cured. The gambling addiction will always remain in the mind of an addicted gambler.

A gambling addiction does not discriminate when it comes to a person's intelligence level. Intellectual or creative thinkers can easily become addicted to gambling, because gambling is a thinking addiction. There is also the competition factor where a gambler wants to beat the odds at the table games or outsmart a high tech programmed computer with the computerized video gambling slot machines.

When an addicted gambler mentally snaps out of their gambling addiction, then they will go a withdrawal period and a deprogramming process. The withdrawal and deprogramming can last for a long time because the mind needs a lot of time to heal from the unhealthy thinking that is caused by the gambling. The goal is for the mind to be restored back to normal sane thinking. As the mind heals then the addicted gambler will get their life back as they get their mind back.

7

SECRETIVE ADDICTION

A gambling addiction is a secretive addiction and is also described as the hidden illness. Many compulsive gamblers have a good job and are dressed nice and are well groomed. A gambler needs to have a good job in order to keep themselves gambling. A lot of gambling is also done in private so as to keep the gambling a secret from their family as well as co-workers.

The majority of gamblers are lonely type of people and their gambling is done in a cocoon of isolation. A gambling machine can be an addicted gamblers best friend and keep them company for many hours until their money is all gone. Lonely gamblers can also make temporary friends at a blackjack table, a poker table, or some other table game.

Compulsive gamblers will not tell other people how much they have lost and will keep this a secret due to the amount of shame and embarrassment that is involved. Gamblers will sometimes tell the world about their gambling winnings, but this is only told to other secretive gamblers. Gambling addicts form some type of a secretive brotherhood.

Gambling addiction is also a hidden disease. This is because the addiction is hidden with the confines of a compulsive or pathological gambler's brain. The disease is internal and lives in the psyche and subconscious realms of the mind. This makes it very easy for an addicted gambler to keep their addiction secretive and hidden until the disease progresses and the awful manifestations of this powerful insidious disease starts to make outward appearances. This happens when the addicted gambler goes through a personality and behavioral change that is negative in nature.

A common personality trait amongst compulsive gamblers is that many of them are shy and introverted. It is very easy for them to go into a gambling environment by themselves and gamble for hours and hours with their best friend the slot machine. They can have the false feeling of being in a social setting with other people. In reality they are isolating alone and are being hypnotized by the slot or video poker machine. An addicted gambler will usually go gamble alone and then go home alone and get upset with themselves about the money that they had just lost.

Many gamblers can stay at home alone and gamble on the internet on their home computer with their credit cards. This is the ultimate form of this secretive addiction. People can now ruin their lives in the convenience of their own home.

There are millions of secretive addicted gamblers in the United States and worldwide. We cannot see that they are compulsive gamblers merely by looking at them. Sooner or later this secretive and hidden addiction becomes revealed and sometimes when it is too late for the addicted gambler.

__ 8 __

PROBLEM GAMBLING

Problem gambling is when a person will gamble a lot and form a secretive addiction and a hidden emotional illness. Gambling at first becomes part of their life but not all of their life. They will do other things for recreation besides gambling. As the addiction progresses then gambling becomes the total focus of a gambler's life and then it becomes a problem. A gambling problem can get worse and progress into a compulsive gambling addiction and then into a pathological gambling addiction.

Most problem gamblers seem to be living a normal life on their outward appearance. They are well dressed and are very good workers because they need the money to support their gambling habit. Internally within their mind is where the insidious gambling addiction resides. This is why a gambling addiction is often referred to as a hidden illness. Problem gambling will affect people of any age, religion, ethnicity, or social background.

Problem gambling is an uncontrollable urge to gamble and a person can also become obsessed with this urge. It is not just the actually gambling playing that is addictive but also the gambling environment and the staff that pushes the free drinks and they also give the gamblers special attention so as to make them feel comfortable so that they will make the casino or bar their second or sometimes first home. Gambling addicts will also form a type of a secret cult society where their god becomes gambling and the casino is their place of worship.

Many problem gamblers will be in somewhat of a mental denial about their addiction to gambling that is at the starting stages. Some will say that there are only recreational gamblers and that they can control their gambling. They will not admit that they are addicted to gambling. This denial becomes stronger as the disease progresses into compulsivity or into a pathological addiction.

There are millions of problem gamblers within the United States and throughout the world. Gambling being accepted as normal behavior is very deceptive. People who start gambling just for fun stand the risk of becoming a problem gambler and getting addicted.

There are several actions that a gambler may perform that could show that they have a gambling problem. The main one is the strong mental denial that problem gamblers possess. The following are other issues that problem gamblers deal with:

Problem gamblers will gamble to escape life's worries or problems.

Problem gamblers will borrow money from credit cards, payday loan companies, pawn shops, or from family or friends to finance their gambling.

Problem gamblers will try to stop gambling several times on their own and are unsuccessful.

Problem gamblers will lie about the amount of time and the amount of money that is spent on their gambling habit.

Problem gamblers will make numerous attempts to win back their losses by chasing their money.

Problem gamblers will experience several episodes of gambler's remorse after losing a lot of money.

Problem gamblers will start to experience depression and negative thoughts and feelings of hopelessness.

Problem gamblers will neglect their physical health by not eating properly or by drinking too much alcohol.

Problem gamblers will seem to be mentally confused due to the cognitive distortion that takes place within a gambler's mind.

__ 9 __

COMPULSIVE GAMBLING

Compulsive gambling is a behavior where a person has to satisfy their strong urge to gamble. A compulsion is not being able to stop doing something. When a person is driven to act out their compulsion, then they have lost control. This is how a gambling addiction can get totally out of control.

Most addicted gamblers feel that they have to gamble. One of the biggest realizations for a recovering gambler is that they do not have to gamble. It is okay to live your life by saving your money instead of throwing the money away in a slot machine, table game, or gambling online on the internet.

Compulsive gamblers are caught up in a progressive illness. The disease can be arrested but not totally healed in the same manner that an alcoholic can stop drinking but will forever be an alcoholic. A person can stop gambling but in a moment of emotional weakness their compulsion to gamble can take over and then they will be back on the self-destructive merry-go-round of throwing their money away.

Compulsive gamblers have an intense mental preoccupation with gambling. It is the mental focus of their lives and is often to the exclusion of other interests or hobbies. Compulsive gamblers are unable to control the amount of money they gamble or the amount of time that is spent gambling.

There are certain characteristics of a compulsive gambler. These are that a compulsive gambler has immaturity, emotional insecurity, and does not want to accept reality.

The immaturity of compulsive gamblers is that they want to have all the good things in life without working hard for them. They want to make easy money by gambling instead of working hard and saving their money. Many compulsive gamblers deceive themselves and perceive their gambling addiction as a part time job. The immaturity also comes when the gambler does not budget or plan their finances.

Compulsive gamblers have a sense of security only when they are actively gambling when in reality they are mostly very insecure persons. Gambling makes them feel important as if they are somebody special. Gambling gives them a false sense of security.

The compulsive gambler does not want to accept reality and as a result they mentally escape into the fantasy world of gambling. Reality is hard to face sometimes because of our personal problems whether they be past, present, or future. Our problems are hard to face and to deal with.

A lot of emotional childhood issues also surface from the subconscious to the conscious mind. An escape into a fantasy world is much more pleasant. The dangerous thing is when a person cannot differentiate between fantasy and reality and it becomes a psychiatric disorder like schizophrenia.

Many compulsive gamblers have experienced trance like disassociation states of mind in which they lose track of time and many gamblers have claimed to have had an out-of-body experience. When addicted gamblers lose track of time then ordinary physical needs take a back seat. A compulsive gambler can go for a long period of time without food, water, or using the restroom.

Compulsive gambling will become a personality disorder and the sick gambler will engage in irrational thinking. This could lead into insanity in which the gambling is performed over and over again with the same result. Performing the same behavior over and over again expecting different results is also the insanity.

Compulsive gambling is an escape into the psyche. The defining characteristic of compulsive gambling is that it is uncontrollable. Compulsive gambling is a step beyond obsession into a personality disorder. Compulsive gambling will progress into pathological gambling, which is an extreme mental, emotional, and personality disorder.

A compulsive gambling addiction is a powerful psychological and behavioral addiction. When this addiction is combined with other addictions like alcohol or drugs then the gambler can really get stuck in an addiction trap. If you also add the sexy cocktail waitresses dressed in revealing costumes and the gambler's need for attention, then the addiction trap becomes stronger.

There is also an addiction to the excitement of the gambling environment whether it is a local bar or a casino. Many compulsive gamblers will gamble so as to get the adrenaline rush. There is more to this insidious disease beside the actually playing.

Gamblers who can gamble in moderation will walk away and go home once they win a lot of money.

Compulsive gamblers will stay gambling until they lose all their money and go home broke and upset.

Compulsive gamblers are in a dream world and they cannot stop the compulsion of their gambling because they want to remain in the dream world. This is why compulsive gamblers can spend hours, months, or years with their mental gambling addiction.

10

MENTAL CONDITIONING

The brain can very easily be mentally conditioned or another way to define this cognitive process is brainwashing. Religious leaders are very good at brainwashing their recruits. The wealthy leaders of the gambling industry are also very good at mentally conditioning their gambling recruits through slick advertising and gimmicks. Once a person becomes a regular patron at a fantasy casino, then they can be brainwashed into a gambling addiction. We must remember that this powerful insidious gambling addiction disease is an addiction of the mind.

Many gambling enterprises employ commercial psychologists to help them design their gambling environment and to help devise methods of how to bring people into their casino to gamble and make a monetary donation to their money making business. It is very easy for a person to get caught up mentally in the fantasy environment of the casino. They can also get caught up with the excitement inside the casino. The mind will also get caught up with the actual gambling and get addicted. The combination of all of these created methods by the casino leaders and commercial psychologists will most certainly get a person's whole being transformed into a gambling addict and become mentally conditioned.

A gambling addiction is a mental addiction and as a result is also an emotional and behavioral addiction. Our behaviors and our actions are controlled by our mental cognitive processes. Gambler's minds can be programmed in the same way that the gambling machines are programmed by a computer. Our minds are also a sophisticated computer. Sooner or later the brainwashed gambler and the slot machine become infused and can become one.

Compulsive addicted gamblers can become mentally conditioned or brainwashed and turn into gambling robots. They will lose mental control of their thinking, emotions, and common sense. Their belief system and mental focus will always be on gambling and the gambling environment. Many addicted gamblers will walk around in a trance as numb robots with no visible emotion. Many of these gambling robots will also become drunk robots with the free alcohol that is freely provide to their minds.

Mind control and brainwashing are not new happenings. The practice of brainwashing and mind manipulation has been taking place ever since the beginning of mankind. People who do not possess a strong self-identity or a healthy perception of reality can very easily be indoctrinated, whether it be religion or gambling. Many addicted gamblers will gamble religiously.

The human mind is a biological computer with software that can be tampered with or contaminated with toxic information. These toxic information will cause a faulty belief system and cognitive distortion. This will as a result cause a lot of mental confusion. We all know the saying; "Garbage in. Garbage out."

The energy and activity of the electronic video poker machines and interactive slot video machines will get ingrained into the brain's memory banks. A mental bonding takes place between the gambling machine and a person's cognitive processes. This mental bonding is what makes a gambling addiction very powerful and hard to break. When a gambler is in the midst of a gambling addiction, they will have the mental perception that their gambling is normal behavior. This is because they are brainwashed and their gambling addiction controls their mind. This is how a gambling addiction can go on for years until the brain snaps out of the mental addiction and starts to get deprogrammed.

There is also the emotional bonding that takes place between a gambler and the gambling environment as well as the friendly bartenders and cocktail waitresses. A gambler's emotions are played upon so as to hook their feelings. A process of conditional love takes place to make the lonely gambler feel important and accepted. This false special attention that is given to gamblers is very powerful because everyone wants to feel wanted and accepted.

The combination of being mentally and emotionally addicted will place a strong hook on a compulsive gambler for years. Gambling becomes an everyday normal way of life and the gambler cannot live without gambling in a friendly fantasy gambling environment.

Probably the most damaging part of the mental conditioning process is the cognitive distortion that takes place in the brain. An addicted gambler who spends hours gambling will have their thought patterns changed and will become confused. In other words the mind can become warped. The result is that affected addicted gamblers will no longer think with a healthy clear mind and will have a distorted perception of reality and will make unhealthy decisions. This cognitive distortion will lead to self-defeating behaviors and self-destruction.

Mental conditioning or brainwashing is a very real personal experience. People can be mentally programmed and as a result have their belief systems and behaviors controlled by an addictive outside force. In order to recover mentally a person has to undergo a deprogramming process to restore their mind back to some form of healthy and sane thinking.

Gambling addiction resides with people's minds. The gambling addiction disease will take control of the subconscious mind and take control of a gambler's everyday thinking. A lot of this thinking turns into negative stinky thinking and is no longer healthy sane thinking. The mind takes on a false perception of reality and their mental perception is one of pure gambling fantasy. A mind can be mentally conditioned or brainwashed and as a result turn a healthy mind into a crazy mind.

11

ESCAPISM

Many addicted gamblers are known as escape gamblers. The goal of escape gamblers is to escape from their boring or dull times in life as well as escaping from personal problems. It is an escape from the real world into a fantasy world that the casinos and gambling bars provide for their patrons. Many lonely people are escape gamblers because they do not want to be home alone.

An escape into the excitement of gambling at a fantasy casino is a lot more pleasant. The problem is that this constant escapism adds to a person's gambling addiction. Today many addicted gamblers can also escape into the various online internet gambling sites on their home computer.

Many people have personal emotional issues and facing the reality of those issues can be very unpleasant and painful. People also have everyday problems that they do not want to deal with. This is why people get involved with various addictions. A gambling addiction is a perfect escape from the reality of everyday personal problems or other life's problems. A fantasy or dream world of gambling in the hopes of winning a jackpot is much more pleasant.

Gambling environments are designed as a place for people to escape to. About 50 million tourists escape to Las Vegas casinos per year. Many of these tourists become addicted to gambling and move to Las Vegas as a permanent escape.

Many compulsive gamblers go through life alone and gambling becomes their best friend. Any single person can escape into the fantasy world of gambling machines or table games at a casino and feel like they are not by themselves. An addicted gambler can spend hours at a casino and not talk to people. They can isolate for hours lost in their mental gambling addiction.

Many of these lonely gamblers become emotionally bonded with the cocktail waitresses or the bartender and feel like they have some real friends. The sad thing is that this false emotionally bonding is conditional friendship and is usually based on the tips that is received from the gambler. The more money that is given as tips to gambling staff then the greater the friendship. These false friendships can be very expensive.

Escapism is prevalent in the gambling world and is a strong part of a compulsive gambling addiction. When our lives are boring and we do not have any positive constructive hobbies, then it is very easy to escape into the fantasy world of gambling.

__ 12 __

THE LOST FOREST

Now that I have stopped gambling, I am recovering from my self-destructive behavior, I am looking back at what I journeyed through. It seems that when my gambling addiction started that I stepped into a forest. As my gambling addiction progressed, I got lost in the forest and this mental forest became a dark lost forest. Today I found my way out of the forest and the sun is shining.

It is very strange that when I was in the middle of the lost forest that my gambling behavior seemed to be normal behavior when it was actually abnormal behavior. I can now see that I spent a lot of time and money in the lost forest.

This lost forest is a state of mind that an addicted gambler enters into. The lost forest seems to have walls on its perimeter, which are the strong walls of denial. Once a gambler is lost in the forest then it is hard to find a way out until they suddenly find an opening and get out of this lost forest state of mind.

When an addicted compulsive gambler is in their lost forest, they lose three basic things, which are time, money, and a sense of values. In the lost forest they are losing valuable time and opportunities that will be gone forever. Also money is becoming lost forever because the gambling world of the lost forest has a very high cost of living. Sense of values also do not exist in the lost forest and especially the value of money. A compulsive gambler can truly get lost in this lost forest state of mind.

Gamblers who are in their lost forest can be easily spotted. They can be seen sitting at a gambling machine for hours and hours. They seem to be in an hypnotic trance lost in their gambling fantasy. Their state of mind has left the real world and they have mentally escaped into the lost forest.

Once a gambler is in their lost forest, then it is very hard to find their way out. People can try to rescue them from the lost forest but many addicted gamblers need to find their own way out of the forest. Hopefully they will find daylight and an opening out of the lost forest before it is too late. Some addicted gamblers choose to remain in the security of the fantasy of the lost forest because they do not want to deal with life outside of the forest.

Deep within the psyche of the subconscious mind is where this lost forest exists. The lost forest is filled with a lot of fog that can be related to the confusion or cognitive distortion that takes place within the mind of an addicted gambler. Once a gambler gets out of their lost forest, then they will describe their emergence or awakening from their gambling addiction as coming out of the fog.

The lost forest is also a fantasy forest and is the dream world of the addicted gambler. Lost in this fantasy state of mind can be life damaging since the gambler is not living within their mind in a state of reality. Their choices in life are made out of pure fantasy and not based on real concrete decisions.

An addicted gambler that is living within the lost forest can look confused and sometimes have several staring episodes due to daydreaming in the fantasy forest. The sick gambler will also sometimes be in a visual trance. The lost forest can be very damaging to a person's mental health.

The end result of being totally lost in the lost forest is mental depression and total withdrawal and isolation from other people and the real world. Many addicted gamblers never get out of their lost forest and will die in the lost forest and many by suicide.

Millions of compulsive or pathological addicted gamblers worldwide are existing in this lost forest and do not know it. The denial that is very strong in the lost forest make an addicted gambler think that they do not have a gambling problem. There is life outside of the lost forest waiting for those gamblers who are mentally lost within the depths of the lost forest. There is a lot of sunshine in the green grass open fields that waits for those gamblers who emerge out of their lost forest state of mind.

__ 13 __

MAGICAL THINKING

Magical thinking for the gambling addict is that the more that they play the greater the odds that they will win the big jackpot and pay off all their bills. Other magical thinking is that they are someone special because they get special treatment by the staff of the gambling environment that they choose to play in.

When the fantasy thinking dominates over reality thinking then that can be referred to as magical thinking. Thoughts of reality enter into the brain's cognitive processes but usually run into a roadblock called denial.

Magical thinking is also when a compulsive gambler is lost in a dream world. They have a dream about winning the big jackpot and becoming rich overnight and being able to provide material things for their family and friends. Addicted gamblers will gamble consistently so as to remain in their dream world and their magical thinking.

This magical thinking is not reality thinking and usually causes the gambler desperation and frustration in search of their gambling dream. It is hard for an addicted gambler to face reality when their magical thinking wears off. The reality of losing money and becoming in financial debt is not fun to deal with. Magical thinking is a lot more pleasant.

The inner child in all of us likes magical thinking. The gambling environment provides an environment for our magical thinking to run wild. Las Vegas is an adult Disney Land created on fantasy and magical thinking. When a person enters the Las Vegas Strip, their inner child goes wild with magical thinking. Casinos play upon this magical thinking and try to make people have a fantasy about gambling and winning a big jackpot.

Magical thinking can become very harmful when it is done in excess. Gambling plays upon our magical thinking and becomes a very important part of a compulsive gambling addiction. Magical thinking is a nice state of mind and is a lot better than reality thinking.

Magical thinking makes us want to think that good things in life happen to us out of a mystical world. In reality we need to make our own magic happen through hard work and making decisions based on reality thinking and not on fantasy or magic.

14

FANTASY WORLD

The majority of people who become gambling addicts have rich fantasy thoughts. Some people live their lives in fantasy and not reality. A fantasy thought is much more pleasant than thoughts dealing with reality. This is why fantasy addictions are so prevalent in our world. Some people use substances like alcohol or other drugs to escape into fantasy and gambling is definitely a mental escape into fantasy.

Those gambling executives who created casinos and other gambling environments have created a fantasy world designed to lure those people who already have a rich fantasy mind set. Millions of people travel to Las Vegas and other gambling meccas just to get lost the gambling fantasy world.

When an addicted gambler enters a gambling environment, they leave reality outside. Reality hits hard when they leave the fantasy world of gambling and go to a home of reality and realize that they threw away $400.00 into a video poker machine and cannot pay their monthly rent.

Compulsive addicted gamblers enter into a dream world of gambling. There is a lot of fantasy dreaming about all the good things they would do with all the money they would win. They would help their families, friends, and the less fortunate. Gamblers also dream about all the nice things that they could buy for themselves.

When a gambler wins a jackpot or a large sum of money, then their fantasy dreams become bigger. When compulsive gamblers are losing money and their fantasy world starts turning into reality then they will spend more money so as to remain in their fantasy world. The dangerous consequence is when a sick gambler can no longer separate fantasy from reality and it become a psychiatric disorder like schizophrenia.

Sick gamblers also have a lot of delusions that help to keep them stuck in their fantasy world. Delusions are irrational beliefs that are maintained despite overwhelming evidence that they have no basis in reality. A gambler can become very delusional especially after they have injected drugs into their brain chemistry like alcohol or narcotics.

There are two major types of conscious fantasy realms. These are realistic fantasy and autistic fantasy. Realistic fantasy is often problem oriented and is most like normal consciousness and helps us solve problems. Autistic fantasy lacks any orientation toward reality.

Addicted gamblers daydream and their conscious or subconscious thinking is in the autistic realm. Once an addicted gambler mentally snaps out of their addiction then they have to deal with realistic fantasy in order to recover mentally, emotionally, and financially from the mess that their powerful gambling addiction had gotten them into.

Coming out of fantasy thoughts and into reality thoughts is the main withdrawal experience that takes place within the mind of a recovering addicted gambler. Feelings and emotions also start to surface along with a lot of psychological pain as part of the withdrawal process. An addicted gambler always living in a fantasy world is numb to their feelings and emotions.

The world of gambling fantasy can really be life damaging not only to themselves but also to their families and friends. Lost in fantasy is what causes compulsive or pathological gamblers to become in financial debt. They lose the concept and value of money and are financially irresponsible. They also do not budget their money and they borrow money to finance their gambling addiction. Credit cards to an addicted gambler lost in their fantasy world become money cards and they do not deal with the reality that they have to pay the money back with interest.

In order to have a healthy financial budget there has to be the three R's, which are responsibility, reality, and restraint. Due to living in a fantasy world, these three R's do not exist for the addicted gambler.

The fantasy world can be crazy making and the fantasy world of the casinos can be crazy making institutions. Extensive gambling for hours and hours and day after day can damage the cognitive processes and can eventually cause a sick gambler to go insane. A healthy person who is mentally sane lives in a world of reality and not in a fantasy world.

15

VALUE OF MONEY

Gambling addicts lose the concept of the value of money and become financially irresponsible. Money turns into play money and there is always the fantasy of winning back the money that is lost gambling. One hundred dollars to a healthy non-gambler goes a long way and could last for a whole week. One hundred dollars to an unhealthy addicted gambler can last from ten minutes to an hour.

Financial priorities of spending money is all mixed up in the warped thinking of the addicted gambler. A gambler will very easily put twenty after twenty into a video poker machine but have a hard time buying clothes for themselves or treating themselves to a good dinner. They want the money for their gambling addiction.

After a few free drinks or beers, the credit cards turn into ATM cards. An addicted gambler will take out several cash advances from their credit cards with no concern that it is borrowed money that has to be paid back and with interest. Usually they will lose the money that they took out from their credit cards. This is known as a double whammy because they have to pay back the lost money. Many gambling addicts are in severe credit card debt. Many credit card companies lose the money when the money is not paid back or the gambler goes into a bankruptcy.

When a gambling addict is lost in their addiction, they are creating financial debt for themselves. They will keep gambling in hopes of winning the money back with a huge jackpot and pay off their bills. This also keeps a gambler hooked and stuck in their gambling disease.

Many addicted gamblers get in debt with payday loan companies, which are legal loan sharks. They have very high interest rates. Many times the gambler will take loans from several of these payday loan companies to pay off each one. These can turn into a vicious cycle of acquired debt.

Pawn shops are also used a lot by addicted gamblers so that they can get money to feed their addiction. Sometimes a sick gambler will steal items that they can go pawn. This is one of the main criminal activities committed by some compulsive gamblers. Another common criminal activity is the writing of bad checks. Their gambling fantasy tells them that they have money in their account when in reality they don't have the money to cover their check.

A gambler that wants to stop gambling has to face the reality of having to pay back their bills. It is much easier to stay lost in their gambling fantasy and remain in denial about their financial mess. The value of money does not exist for the addicted gambler until they snap out of their mental addiction and restore their mind back to some normalcy of healthy thinking.

__ 16 __

CHASING YOUR LOSSES

When a gambler loses money, then they will use their ATM card, credit cards or take out personal loans to get more money in order to play and get their lost money back. This is called chasing your losses or chasing your money and could last for hours, days, weeks, or even years.

The period of chasing your lost money is a period of insanity because the addicted gambler is doing the same thing over and over again expecting a different result. Sick gamblers will chase their losses until their money is all gone and they need to continue chasing their money. Chasing your money is like being on a merry-go-round and not being able to get off.

The dangerous part of chasing your losses is the need to borrow money in order to try and win back the money that was lost. The easiest way to borrow money is to get cash advances from credit cards. Many compulsive gamblers do not want to realize that getting money from credit cards is borrowing money with interest that has to be paid back.

As a result many addicted gamblers get into credit card abuse and get themselves into severe financial debt. This credit card debt will ruin people's lives and they will spend years paying off their credit cards. Many gamblers will have no choice but to file bankruptcy to eliminate their debt.

Another way to borrow quick money is to get money from payday loan companies. The interest rates are very high at these loan shark companies. Many addicted gamblers will take out loans from several payday loan companies and get themselves in extreme debt. They will use one loan to try and pay off another loan.

Many gamblers will spend their whole pay-checks just trying to break even. They usually lose their hard earned paycheck and then borrow money and get themselves in debt. It is ironic that the process of chasing your losses only gets an addicted gambler deeper in debt, which is what they are trying to avoid. This proves that the thinking of compulsive or pathological gamblers is warped.

During this phase of insanity, a sick gambler can lose total control of how much money is being tossed away into gambling machines, table games, or on the internet. As a result a compulsive gambler can chase their money until their money is all gone and they are broke.

__ 17 __

OBSESSION AND POSSESSION

An obsession involves not being able to stop thinking about something, and a compulsion involves not being able to stop doing something. An obsession is thought that recurs again and again, despite attempts to stop or block it.

Many gamblers who are obsessed with their gambling behavior also seem to become possessed psychologically and spiritually. The mental gambling addiction has a very strong grip on a person's whole being, which includes their thoughts, emotions, and spirit.

Obsession and possession are closely corre-lated to one another. A gambler gets obsessed about gambling and then will eventually become possessed by their powerful gambling addiction. Their obsession makes them go into a gambling environment on a regular basis, which puts them in an environment where they can be possessed. The possession takes place when their minds get brainwashed and controlled by the totality of their gambling addiction experience.

We are all spiritual beings living inside human bodies. There is the saying that money is the root of all evil. We can give into the seductive temptation of gambling and then become spiritually possessed. We then have to pay the consequence of giving into the temptation of the gambling temptation.

Being spiritually possessed by gambling is real and a compulsive gambler can get involved in a spiritual bondage or another way to describe this is being locked up inside a spiritual prison. It is hard to break out of this spiritual prison because besides our human spirit being possessed our minds and emotions are also locked up inside the gambling prison within our minds.

Having this strong possession by gambling is what makes a gambling addiction to be the hardest addiction to break free from. The obsession and possession by gambling takes control of the mind and can cause psychiatric disorders. For many addictive gamblers it takes years to break free from the powerful obsession and possession with gambling.

We can go into any casino or gambling environment and see many compulsive or pathological gamblers sitting at slot machines for several hours. They seem to be hypnotized and lost in a mental trance. Most of these sick gamblers also have a frown on their face and do not look like they are having fun gambling. They are lost in their spiritual gambling prison.

Once an addicted compulsive gambler gets out of being spiritually possessed then the obsession to gamble will also leave. The compulsion to gamble will leave but will always be within a gambler's mind and soul. It is very possible for an addicted gambler to once again become obsessed and possessed by gambling.

The gambling addiction disease can be arrested but never cured completely. This is why it is important to be involved with a support group comprised of other compulsive gamblers. It will take several years to recover from the tight grip of gambling that has gambler's minds possessed. The obsession to gamble will also decrease after years of abstinence from gambling.

18

PATHOLOGICAL GAMBLING

Pathological gambling is when gambling addiction becomes more than problem or compulsive gambling and becomes a life destructive mental psychiatric disorder. A person's gambling integrates into a person's cognitive processes and takes over the fantasy side of the brain. The addicted gambler no longer has healthy sane thinking but only thinks of gambling and escaping into their gambling fantasy world.

The definition of pathological gambling in psychiatric terms is: "A persistent, recurrent maladaptive gambling behavior that disrupts personal, family, or vocational pursuits." As with all addictions, pathological gambling may even have neuro-chemical aspects in the brain that could be genetic.

Pathological gambling is a progressive disorder that involves impulse and control problems. The consequences of pathological gambling can be devastating to the person's family and career.

The psychological disorder of pathological gambling can be treated by mental health professionals. Most mental health workers will advise that addicted gamblers attend support group meetings such as twelve step anonymous groups.

The term pathological gambling is an impulse control disorder and compulsive gambling is a compulsion to gamble. Pathological gambling also includes an obsessive-compulsive disorder. Many problem gamblers and compulsive gamblers transform into pathological gamblers when they mentally cross the line where they lose total control of their gambling addiction disease.

The combination of impulse control and obsessive-compulsive mental disorders as well as not separating fantasy from reality can cause serious mental damage. The pathological gambler has a very unhealthy degree of sanity and prolonged pathological gambling can lead to insanity.

There are also a lot of ups and downs or highs and lows. These mood swings can be extensive and to the extremes. An addicted gambler can have a high euphoria state of mind when they are winning and then their mood can swing to an extreme low and depression when they realize how much money they have lost. Gambling addicts can also suffer from a manic-depressive disorder.

Pathological gambler's minds can get lost in a blind spot and they cannot see the problem that they have created for themselves. This is when an addicted gambler enters into what I call the lost forest state of mind as discussed in an earlier chapter.

Gamblers caught up in this extreme stage of addiction will make decisions with their emotions and not logical rational thinking. That is why a pathological gambler makes many mental mistakes that they will regret later. This happens when a sick gambler wakes up from their gambling addiction and starts to come out of their mental fog of the lost forest, which is the journey from insanity back to sanity.

Addicted pathological gamblers can get lost in their addiction for several years. This psychiatric disorder becomes very powerful and controls a person's thinking processes as well as their emotions. The end result is that gambling for a sick pathological gambler seems to become normal behavior and a common way of life. The pathological gambler loses their mind to gambling and possible insanity awaits them if they do not snap out of their powerful mental addiction of the mind. Usually it is a rude awakening when a gambler mentally wakes up from their addiction.

Some of the major characteristics of a pathological gambler is that they are preoccupied with gambling. The gambler also needs to gamble with higher amounts of money, gets restless or irritable when trying to stop, gambles to escape reality, chases lost money, lies to family members, performs illegal acts, destroys work or personal relationships, borrows money for a bailout from debts, and has repeated unsuccessful efforts to try to stop gambling.

People who already have some type of mental issues like being bipolar or some degree of schizophrenia are strong candidates for a pathological gambling addiction. Others simply have addictive personalities and can also be involved with other addictions at the same time. The gambling industry leaders take advantage of these people who are not in possession of a healthy sane mind but who prefer to live in a fantasy state of mind.

19

SELF-DEFEATING BEHAVIOR

Self-defeating behavior is behavior that is destructive to a person's life instead of enhancing their life. A good definition of self-defeating behavior is:

A true self-defeating behavior is an action or attitude that once worked to help an individual to cope with a hurtful experience but now works against the individual to keep them from responding to new moments of life in a healthy way.

There are many behaviors that we do in order to bring self-destruction to our lives instead of doing positive behaviors that bring us happiness and success. Some of these negative behaviors that we act out that are related to a gambling addiction are lying, smoking, drinking alcohol, taking drugs, manipulating others, procrastinating, stealing, spending money one does not have, and gambling. A lot of the self-defeating behaviors are also self-punishment and self-abuse. A lot of these thoughts and behaviors are from the subconscious part of the mind.

In her book, "From Surviving To Thriving," Mary Bratton writes:

Other forms of self-punishment and self-abuse are more subtle. Echoing the risk-taking behavior of a self-abusive child, adult survivors drive too fast, shop compulsively, gamble excessively, and have unexplained accidents. Living life on the edge, surrounded by self-created chaos, survivors seem to be repeating all that they struggled to escape.

There are three major characteristics that all self-defeating behaviors share. The characteristics are that at one point or another, a self-defeating behavior had worked to help an individual deal with a hurtful or threatening situation. Another characteristic is that a self-defeating behavior is never the behavior that should be used in a particular situation. The third characteristic is that a self-defeating behavior guarantees the consequences that the individual is trying to avoid in practicing the self-defeating behavior.

Self-defeating behaviors or thoughts are destructive, dangerous, and deceptive. They come into our lives as friends that helped us cope with traumatic events or other hurtful events growing up as children into adolescence. Later on in life as adults they reveal themselves as enemies that will cause self-destruction and misery. Many of these self-destructive patterns also become active in the tough teenage years.

These self-defeating behaviors can take on many forms. The two main categories where these behaviors take place are in our inward thoughts and our outward behaviors. A major effect of gambling addiction and self-defeating thoughts is that our thinking becomes warped and we usually come up with faulty mental conclusions that are not real in nature. Our warped thoughts then cause us to act out warped behaviors.

The following are examples of these self-defeating techniques. This list is derived from the book by Milton R. Cudney, Ph.D. and Robert E. Hardy, Ed.D. entitled "Self-Defeating Behaviors."

Alcohol Abuse	Fantasizing
Drug Abuse	Blanking One's Mind
Lying	Reviewing Past Hurts
Being Sarcastic	Intellectualizing
Smoking	Rationalizing
Procrastination	Selective Forgetting
GAMBLING	False Limitations
Stealing	Negative Results
Acting Crazy	Holding Feelings
Pouting	Imposing Guilt
Being Late	Magnifying Problems

The price that we pay for practicing these various self-defeating thoughts or behaviors are the following:

Loneliness	Anxiety	Shame
Helplessness	Alienation	Sadness
Bitterness	Humiliation	Guilt
Rage	Hatred	Self-Esteem

20

LIFE'S CONSEQUENCES

Gambling addiction not only has a negative effect on a person' life financially, but also affects every facet of a person's life. Addictive gamblers are focused only on gambling and their lives are controlled by their addiction. They are not living life but are existing in life as an emotionless zombie robot. There are definitely high points and low points and the end consequence for a compulsive or pathological gambler that does not snap out of their addiction is death, insanity, or prison.

There are several life's consequences for the personal addicted gambler that are life damaging. There are also societal consequences that deal with personal economics and societal economics. The main thing is that the addicted gambler who gets in financial debt affects not only themselves but also their families and also society as a whole.

Gambling addicts are financially irresponsible and do not deal with financial reality. They do no save money but instead spend their paychecks and get in debt with credit cards, personal loans, or payday loan companies. Many spend the rest of their lives recovering from their financial debt. Bankruptcy rates are very high amongst compulsive gamblers.

Financial banks, credit card companies, and other financial institutions suffer a loss in revenue due to bankruptcies and home foreclosures. Many compulsive addicted gamblers are not able to pay off their extensive debt they created during their gambling days. Many compulsive gamblers end up owing the Internal Revenue Service thousands of dollars and some end up in prison for tax fraud.

Some addicted gamblers will engage in criminal activities. Many will write bad checks without having the money in their bank account to cover the check amount. Gamblers will deplete their bank accounts by continuously taking money out of an ATM machine. A major financial mistake is taking out cash advances from their credit cards. Keeping track of the balance of their bank accounts or even credit cards is not common for addicted gamblers.

Other gamblers will steal money or steal material items that they can take to a pawn shop for money. Some addicted gamblers will also embezzle money from the company they work for or from their personal business. Other criminal activities that some gamblers get involved in are robbery, assault, and prostitution. They will do anything to get money to feed their gambling addiction.

Many compulsive gamblers end up in a hospital emergency room with health issues directly related to their gambling addiction. In Las Vegas the hospitals report that an average of 30 people visit emergency rooms daily and they are compulsive gamblers.

Many of these people have attempted suicide or have harmed other people as a result of a bad day of gambling. Others suffer anxiety attacks or heart attacks. Some overdose on alcohol or drugs and also end up in a regular hospital while some end up in a mental hospital. Others end up in car accidents after they are very upset and angry after losing a lot of money to gambling.

The doctors do not write down gambling as a reason for the medical emergency. Because like politicians they also support gambling because gambling also brings them a lot of business dollars. When a sick gambler commits suicide, the death is reported as natural and not that the person died as a result of major depression related to their gambling addiction.

This chapter was titled life's consequences because the consequences of a compulsive or a pathological gambling addiction carries a life sentence. It takes a long time for the addicted gambler to recover back to financial health, physical health, and emotional health. For many gamblers it is easy to stay in their gambling disease instead of facing the reality of the painful recovery from the damage they have caused to themselves and their families.

Many compulsive gamblers will not just lose their homes but will also lose their family members due to divorce and become alone and isolated. They will miss the valuable time that they did not spend with their families. While an addicted gambler is spending most of their personal time gambling, life happens around them. The divorce rate is high in marriages where one or both spouses are gambling addicts. Children always suffer when a divorce takes place.

The sad part is that many compulsive or pathological gamblers end up homeless for life. The combination of losing their money, their sanity, and their self-esteem keeps many gamblers homeless. A powerful gambling addiction can drive a person crazy. This addiction of the mind will warp the brain chemistry and thought processes. Getting lost in a fantasy world and not living in reality is a major part of the loss of mental sanity that addicted gamblers experience.

There are many homeless former millionaires surviving on the streets of Las Vegas and other cities where there is a gambling industry.

The ultimate life consequence is that suicide is the only option for many sick addicted gamblers. In Las Vegas many hopeless depressed addicted gamblers will overdose at home or in a hotel room. Others will jump off of a building or a parking garage. Many will simply take a gun and shoot themselves or take a knife and slit their neck or wrist. There are some cases where an addicted gambler has hung themselves with casino hotel room bed sheets. These gambling suicides are rarely or never mentioned in the news media because the major advertisers for the news media outlets happen to be in the gambling industry.

Once a sick addicted gambler realizes of how their gambling addiction has affected their life as well as their families lives then they will usually hit bottom and hopefully begin their lifelong recovery process. It may take years to recover from the harmful life consequences of a compulsive or pathological gambling addiction of the mind.

21

HITTING BOTTOM

Most addicted gamblers do not wake up from their gambling addiction until they reach an emotional bottom. Some gamblers hit bottom when they have a strong realization of how their compulsive gambling behavior has affected their finances, job performance, or family relationships. Sometimes it is a combination of all three.

Hitting an emotional bottom happens when a addicted gambler's dream world of gambling comes face to face with a big dose of reality. This can be a very tough emotional period for a compulsive or pathological gambler who has been in their gambling addiction for a long period of time. They suddenly come to realizations about how their negative self-destructing gambling behavior was destroying their life. Addicted gamblers will also experience a lot of incomprehensible demoralization, which can be unbearable at times.

The sad thing is that it takes some compulsive gamblers to hit their emotional bottom to stop their gambling and move forward in life in a more positive way. A lot of the time the financial and personal damage has already been done when the gambler hits their emotional bottom. There will be a lot of anxiety and possible depression during this period of time. Also there will be a lot of debt anxiety present has the addict starts to come out of denial and realizes the amount of debt that they have accumulated.

A sad statistic is that many compulsive gamblers will commit suicide when they hit their emotional bottom and are forced to face a harsh reality. A gambler that hits this bottom can also become very angry and can act out in violent behavior and hurt other people or commit criminal acts and end up in prison. Some may also lose their sanity and end up in a mental hospital. There are professional out-patient clinics that are ran by medical mental professionals that can help an addicted gambler journey through this stage of hitting an emotional bottom.

Once an addicted gambler hits bottom, then the only way is to look up. Sometimes we all need to go through a valley to reach the mountain top. The valley will not be a pleasant valley. Snapping out of a powerful mental gambling addiction is a rude awakening and can be a battle between insanity and sanity.

Gambling addicts who hit their emotional bottom will become very emotional. During their gambling career they were emotion less zombies. The most common emotions that will emerge are anger and crying. Hitting bottom is also the beginning of a grieving process concerning the lost time and lost money. There will also be restless or sleepless nights and sometimes nightmares will also take place. The gambling ghosts will try to maintain control of the minds of the addicted gamblers and try to keep them in their gambling addiction. These gambling ghosts do not want an addicted gambler to recover by their mind being restored back to healthy clear sane thinking.

After experiencing an emotional bottom is when the withdrawal symptoms start to happen. Gambling has caused the mind to exercise abnormal thinking, which relates to the abnormal gambling behavior. The gambling withdrawal symptoms can be severe at times and the most common symptoms are depression and isolation. It is very important for the sick gambler to be around people and a good place is by attending meetings at a twelve-step program designed to help compulsive gamblers recover from this insidious disease.

Prolonged depression and loneliness can cause a gambler to go deeper into an emotional valley where they could possibly cause self-destruction to themselves. It is possible to head for the mountain top and begin the long climb upward and out of their powerful mental gambling addiction that has had a tight grip on their mind, soul, and spirit.

__ 22 __

RUDE AWAKENING

Hitting the emotional bottom is the first step toward recovery from a gambling addiction and this period can be referred to as a rude awakening. This rude awakening happens when an addicted gambler finally breaks through the mental roadblock of denial and comes out of the fantasy of the lost forest and comes face to face with reality.

The transition from fantasy magical thinking to reality thinking is a very harsh mental and emotional experience. Coming to terms with reality is very hard but is necessary toward becoming mentally and emotionally healthy again. The first step during this rude awakening period is to admit that a gambling problem does exist and has to be dealt with.

This awakening is like waking up from a coma-tose mental state of mind where the mind's focus was only on gambling and spending time in a gambling environment. An addicted gambler will also take a look at the past events of their gambling career and may experience a lot of regret and emotional pain. The main thing is that they are mentally snapping out of their gambling addiction.

An addicted compulsive or pathological gambler can be in a hypnotized gambling state of mind for years. Gambling being an addiction of the mind can take control of a gambler's whole being. The rude awakening begins the recovery journey from insanity back to sanity.

RECOVERY

Recovery from a mental and behavioral gambling addiction is a slow process. The gambler needs to recover mentally, emotionally, and needs to mend past family issues. The best way to recover is to share your recovery with other recovering compulsive gamblers. A good safe place to do this is by attending several meetings at an anonymous twelve-step program that deals with compulsive gambling addiction. There are also outpatient treatment programs with mental health professionals if an addicted gambler needs personal therapy.

A twelve-step anonymous recovery program is also a fellowship where one can make friends and learn again to socialize with other people. By the group therapy that is provided in a twelve-step program, the addicted compulsive gamblers help each other to go forward in their personal recovery process. There is an atmosphere in which a lonely gambler can learn to relate and not isolate. The majority of compulsive or pathological gamblers spend hours alone gambling. Recovery is a chance to start living life again instead of existing.

Since a gambling addiction is an addiction of the mind, an addicted gambler needs to change their thought processes in order to get their mind back that was lost to gambling. Once a gambler's thinking changes then their behaviors will also change. The major goal is to recognize negative thoughts and turn them into positive thoughts and as a result positive actions and behaviors.

Once an addicted gambler stops gambling, then they are left with a thinking and living problem. It is necessary to search inward and discover what it is within their soul and mind that got them into their powerful insidious gambling addiction. Many times a person is carrying mental and emotional luggage from their childhood that has not been dealt with. Once a person deals with these painful issues then they can be free from their past and go move on with their life. It is very important that in recovery to live one day at a time and to live and think in the present.

There are some psychological and emotional withdrawal symptoms that emerge when a gambler is coming out of their gambling addiction. The hardest part is the psychological and emotional pain that has to be endured in order to get back their real self and regain their healthy cognitive processes and healthy emotions.

There is an adjustment period coming out of a mental addiction and it is often described as coming out of the fog. Eventually a gambler's perception will change and their thinking will become clearer and sharper. Our perception is our reality so as our mental perception changes for the better than so does our reality and we act accordingly in a more positive way.

A recovering gambler will have a lot of restlessness. There will be some insomnia with sleepless nights at first. The addicted gambler might wake up in the middle of the night and have to experience some tough psychological and emotional pain. The body is trying to return back to normalcy. It is important to note that the recovery process is not the same for all addicted gamblers but there are a lot of similarities.

Letting go of the past can be hard to do when a recovering gambler realizes about the time and money that was lost during the period of their life that was consumed by their gambling addiction. The lost time and lost opportunities will be regretted. The lost money can be regained and new life opportunities can be explored. A healthy sane mind is priceless.

Recovery can be a slow and hard process to have to go through for an addicted gambler. There is a good life awaiting the gambler as they get their mind and life back. The gambler in recovery needs to find their real self that was masked by their gambler false self. One the real self starts to emerge than good positive self-esteem starts to return.

A major part of recovery is for a gambler to regain back their self-esteem and get their life back. For many months or years gambling has controlled their lives and they have been a slave to their addiction. As the illness of the gambling addiction progresses then the gambling addict loses their self-esteem and sometimes they gamble to self-defeat themselves or subconsciously they punish themselves.

Recovery can be a very hard and trying time for a person coming out of a powerful gambling addiction. It takes a lot of strong character to endure the emotional pain that has to be endured in order to return to a healthy state of mind and good emotional health.

A gambling addiction, whether it may be compulsive or pathological, can cause cognitive distortion within the minds of addicted gamblers. This means that the thought processes have been distorted or warped.

This will, as a result, cause mental, emotional, psychological, and personality disorders in addicted gamblers. Recovery from the combination of these disorders will take some time.

As the mind recovers, there will be a lot of anxiety. Emotions will surface such as anger and crying. The recovering gambler will go through a grieving process as they grieve their gambling days. The recovering gambler will most likely also be in financial debt so there will also be a lot of debt anxiety. This is the part of the recovery process when it is time to start focusing on the solution and not the problem.

The majority of addicted gamblers have experienced some form of childhood trauma or other traumatic events that could have occurred in adolescence or adulthood. Gambling has been an escape from hurtful feelings or emotions. In order to get healthy, the recovering gambler needs to work through these toxic memories and emotions in order to be free from the past.

During recovery, a lot of these hurtful memories and feelings will enter the conscious realm and will cause a lot of emotional pain. The subconscious mind has no sense of chronological time. Traumatic events that occurred several years earlier will appear in the conscious mind in present time and the person will be experiencing these traumatic events as if they are happening also in the present. Crying is a very good emotional release that will help a person get past these past traumatic events as they re-experience them and then let them go.

Gambling recovery is a growing up process. The inner child has been damaged due to past traumatic events that were out of their control. This turns the adult into an irresponsible adult. Most of the time it is the irresponsible inner child that becomes the addicted gambler. A mature adult does not throw their hard earned money away to gambling. The maturation process is from an irresponsible inner child to a mature adult. The mature adult makes positive self-enhancing decisions instead of self-defeating or self-destructing decisions.

Compulsive or pathological gamblers have a chance for a good life by going through recovery from this insidious gambling disease. Recovery happens when an addicted gambler transforms from self-hate to self-love.

The gambling disease can be placed in remission but can never be completely cured. There will always be that gambling devil on the recovering gamblers shoulder always tempting them to gamble their money away.

A very important part of recovery and restoration to a healthy and sane mind is to have spirituality become part of a recovering addicted gambler's life. Spirituality is having a personal relationship with a god or a higher power of our own understanding. There is a difference between spirituality and religion. Religion is for those people trying to escape hell and spirituality is for those who have already been there. Going to church is good but addicts need to be careful that they don't take on a religious addiction and get involved in a toxic cult.

Denial is a very strong psychological obstacle that stands in the way of the mental recovery for an addicted gambler in recovery. An addicted gambler has a hard time admitting to themselves or to others that they have a gambling problem. The compulsive gambler will say that they are gambling just to have fun or to relax. The diseased mind of an addicted gambler will think of all kinds of excuses for their gambling addiction.

There is also societal denial about the gambling disease epidemic. The casino industry keeps promoting gambling has normal behavior. Problem and compulsive gambling is kept hidden and is not exposed as the crazy making abnormal behavior that it is. The goal is to keep gambling addiction as a hidden and secretive disease.

The first step to recovery for the gambling addiction worldwide or for the individual addicted gambler is to break down the strong walls of denial. In order to recover from this insidious powerful life damaging and societal damaging disease is to honestly admit that there is a problem that needs to be faced head on.

__ 24 __

MY PERSONAL EXPERIENCE

A few years before I moved to Las Vegas, Nevada from Albuquerque, New Mexico, a relative and I were in Las Vegas for a day. We were at a convenience store and I observed a lady sitting at a video poker machine. She was totally immersed in the gambling machine and she seemed to be in a hypnotic trance. I told my relative, "Look at that lady. Isn't that crazy." Well, a few years later I became that lady and joined her as a fellow compulsive addicted gambler.

About eight years ago, I started playing video poker at a local bar just for fun and to pass some time. The game was fun and the pretty female bartender was very friendly and nice to me. She kept giving me free beers while I was gambling. What a deal. I played some songs on the jukebox and was having a good time. Spending time at the gambling bar was a lot more fun that being home alone watching television.

Many days after work I would escape to a local gambling bar and this became a habitual occurrence. I wanted to be amongst friendly people who would call me by my first name. The more tips that I would give the bar staff then the more friendlier they would be with me.

It was at these local corner gambling bars where my gambling addiction got started. I soon ventured to the Las Vegas Strip and started playing slot machines and once in a while a table game. My favorite slot machine was the video poker machines, which are the most addicting gambling game. I would win money sometimes and once in a long while I would win a jackpot, which gave me more money to play with. My first jackpot was a royal flush for a thousand dollars.

I was hooked.

My gambling addiction started to take hold of my mind and I would spend many hours gambling at corner bars and on the Las Vegas Strip. Many times I would lose track of time and I would gamble all night. My denial about having a gambling problem was also in my mindset because I would tell myself that I was only playing for fun.

I would lose money all time and many times it was more than a hundred dollars. When I would finally leave the fantasy world of gambling and return back to the real world when I entered my apartment, I would realize what I did and get mad at myself. This is called gamblers remorse.

The next day I would go gamble again to try to win my money back. I started to chase my money and then I got on the gambling merry-go-round and it was hard to get off. My gambling addiction became stronger when I started to chase my money losses.

Gambling became a way of life for me. Gambling seemed to be normal behavior to me when it is really abnormal behavior. I felt that I had to gamble and today I realize that I do not have to gamble.

Sometimes I would gamble all night long and go home when the sun came up. The way that I knew that I was there all night was when the bar staff or casino cocktail waitresses had a shift change. Many times I would go home and get a couple hours of sleep and then go to work. A positive thing was that I was a good employee during my gambling and I still am today. My job was very important because I needed the money to feed my gambling addiction and then later to pay debt that I accumulated because of my gambling.

Gambling consumed my mind and my total person. My life was focused on getting that jackpot or chasing my money and of course I enjoyed getting the free drinks. I would not date or go on vacations. I was married to the video poker machines. My addiction got worse and I went from a problem gambler to a compulsive gambler. Later on in my addiction I crossed the line and became a pathological gambler and I lost control of my gambling and my gambling addiction controlled my mind.

Many times I would leave my credit cards and ATM cards at home. I would try to set a monetary limit and only gamble with a certain amount of cash that I had in my wallet. When my money was gone I would go home and get my money cards so that I can continue playing.

As an addictive gambler, I got to the place in my mind where I could no longer comprehend the value of money. Real money turned into play money. After a few free beers my credit cards would turn into ATM cards. I was never able to save money and I was surviving from paycheck to paycheck. At the same time I was running up debt on my many credit cards.

Now that I have stopped gambling and am re-covering from my mental gambling addiction, I feel stupid that I ever started gambling. How could a rational college educated person as myself get deeply involved in a gambling addiction. Many addicted gamblers happen to be intelligent people with good jobs. Gambling addiction does not discriminate when it come to ethnic status, social status, or intelligence quotient.

Waking up from my gambling addiction was a rude awakening. I had to face reality and had to deal with a lot of childhood emotional and psychological issues. I have also come to understand how I was set up for a gambling addiction as well as my former religious addiction. In order to recover emotionally, I had to deal with emotional scars or traumatic events from my past.

I came from a very traumatic childhood that caused my inner child to go hide deep within my soul in order to survive. My mind at this young age also formed a rich imaginary and fantasy world. My childhood fantasies helped me survive as a toddler. In my adulthood the fantasy world that I had as a kid helped get me into my gambling addiction and my former religious addiction. Both addictions are mind and fantasy addictions.

My early childhood years were spent homeless surviving on the streets of Albuquerque. We would sleep at the bus depot or in hotel restrooms and sometimes we would not sleep at all. In the daytime we would stand outside the bars and beg for money. Sometimes my sister and I would dance for the bar patrons for tips.

My mother was a very quiet person so we grew up in a quiet world and did not learn the necessary communication or social skills. My mother also did not let us play with other kids, which also did not allow us to become social people. As a result I grew up to be introverted and a loner. The majority of compulsive gamblers are lonely introverts who isolate and do not relate to people.

During my elementary school years, my sister and I lived in several foster homes. We were used as child labor in some of the foster homes, especially our first foster home which was a ranch. Since I was already a shy introverted kid, I was bullied at school and by other children in the foster homes. This only caused my inner child to go deeper into hiding inside my psyche. The world was not a good safe place to live so I learned that emotional isolation was a good place to live in.

During my adolescent years, I was also mistreated by my male cousin and his friends. I was physically and emotionally abused and was a shy teenager. I would always hide from people because I was afraid that they would hurt me.

As a result of the emotional trauma in my life, I grew up with low self-esteem and an inferiority complex. I also grew up with a huge void in my inner person and was starving for love and attention.

As an young adult, I found conditional love in a toxic religious cult and assumed a religious addiction. My religious addiction was also a fantasy addiction of the mind in a similar manner that gambling addiction is.

The same way that I was religious about my religion; I was religious about my gambling addiction.

As an addicted gambler, I could sit at a video poker machine or slot machine and isolate for several hours at a time. I was given a lot of conditional attention by the bartenders and sexy cocktail waitresses. They made me feel special and important.

Much of this conditional love was based upon the amount of tips that I gave them for my free drinks.

My free drinks allowed me to come out of my shyness and I was able to socialize with other gamblers. The gambling environment allowed gamblers to come together and pretend to be buddies when in reality they are in the most part lost lonely souls.

The combination of receiving special attention and sometimes winning jackpots of money got me hooked. The money that I would win would eventually go back into the video poker machine. Whenever I was feeling lonely or sad, I could escape into the fantasy world of gambling. Eventually gambling became a way of life and my gambling addiction became stronger until I hit bottom and had my rude awakening.

I totally got lost in the lost forest of gambling and could not find my way out. Until one night I saw an opening to the outside of the lost forest. I walked out of the fantasy forest state of mind and entered into a valley of reality. I had a rude awakening and I faced reality face to face. I faced myself in my bathroom mirror with tears in my eyes and said to myself, "Mike, what in the hell are you doing!"

It was a big shock coming out of the fantasy world of my powerful insidious gambling addiction and into the real world. A lot of fear and anxiety started to pop up at various times during the days and especially at night when I was trying to sleep. I would wake up in the middle of the night very emotional and I would cry and get angry. My recovery process within my mind was getting me back in touch with my feelings and emotions.

My feelings and emotions were starting to surface after being numbed for several years when my gambling addiction had control on my mind, soul, and spirit. My withdrawal symptoms were very real as my mind and body were trying to be restored back to normalcy.

I was set up for my gambling addiction and other addictions as a result of my traumatic childhood. In the book, "Trauma And Addiction," by Tian Dayton she writes, "Unresloved and untreated childhood trauma is a primary cause of addiction and relapse. Self-medicating with substance such as drugs, alcohol and behaviors like sex, gambling or frenetic activity masquerades as a solution to pain but carries a deep human cost."

There were days when I was feeling terrible within my person but I still had to go to work and perform. After three months from when I stopped gambling, I realized that I needed help to recover from my powerful gambling addiction. I then humbled myself and started going to twelve-step anonymous meetings that dealt with gambling addiction. At the meetings were a lot of people just like me that got caught up in an insidious gambling addiction.

My recovery started to move forward and it has been almost two years that I have not placed a bet. At the present time I am living life again and learning to relate and not isolate. It is a very good feeling to wake up in the morning and realize that I do not have to gamble today.

The following are the various steps of my personal gambling addiction experience:

1. Got a good paying job.

2. Started playing video poker for fun.

3. Won some jackpots.

4. Gambling environment was exciting.

5. Friendly cocktail waitress and bar staff.

6. Started losing a lot of money.

7. Gamble again to win money back.

8. Chasing my losses merry-go-round.

9. Use cash advances from credit cards.

10. Lose the concept and value of money.

11. Start getting into financial debt.

12. Compulsive gambling takes over.

13. Self-destructing behavior continues.

14. Living in a dream fantasy world.

15. Start having emotional episodes.

16. Hit bottom and have rude awakening.

17. Start coming out of the mental fog.

18. Realize the stupidity of my behavior.

19. Recovery stage and group meetings.

20. Start living life one day at a time.

21. Live life without gambling.

25

THE NEED FOR GREED

COMMENTARY

Gambling was created and designed to take your money. The goal of the leaders of the gambling industry is to become wealthy at the expense of the sick addicted compulsive or pathological gambler. Gamblers are encouraged and welcomed to spend time at the casinos and other gambling establishments as long as they are donating money into the bank account of the respective gambling business. As long as the gambler is gambling they will receive unlimited free drinks. The corporate leaders that created the gambling industry as it is today are very greedy and they have the need for greed.

Las Vegas is a desert. The casinos located on the Las Vegas Strip are a created adult fantasy oasis where the fantasy of becoming instantly wealthy by hitting a jackpot is advertised and promoted worldwide. As a result, about 50 million people visit Las Vegas per year. The number of gambling visitors that visit other gambling resorts combined worldwide is astronomical and is probably in the billions.

The number of compulsive or pathological gamblers that are created by the worldwide gambling industry is also in the millions. Probably the greatest concentration of addicted gamblers is located in the Las Vegas, Nevada area and in southern California. There are several casinos in California and millions of Californians make the trip yearly to Las Vegas to satisfy their gambling addiction. Compulsive gamblers in the United States and worldwide also have the need for greed.

Las Vegas, Atlantic City, and Macau, China as well as other gambling meccas are fun cities to visit. They offer a lot more to do during a vacation besides gambling. The problem is that the main focus of these gambling resorts is gambling. They would not survive or flourish if it was not for the money that is taken from the addicted compulsive or pathological gambler.

A few blocks from the Strip casinos in Las Vegas is the real world where the poor, homeless, and the less fortunate of society are surviving on the streets. In southern Nevada there are about 11,000 homeless people at any given time. There is so much money in Las Vegas that is accumulated by the gambling industry that there should not be a homeless problem in Las Vegas. Many of the homeless in Las Vegas are addicted gamblers who have lost all their money and ended up at the bottom and are surviving one day at a time.

I have lived in Las Vegas, Nevada for 13 years and I have observed a lot regarding the gambling industry and gambling environment that never stops. The gambling industry in Las Vegas is very similar to other gambling industries worldwide. In fact many of the gambling casinos in other parts of the world have been created by Las Vegas casino corporations. Macau, China is going to be a bigger gambling resort than Las Vegas, Nevada.

Gambling addiction does not discriminate regarding race, ethnic background, gender, religion, social status, or intelligence level. My personal gambling addiction almost destroyed my life. This insidious evil addiction of the mind had control of my mind, soul, and spirit for several years. I am thankful that I was able to snap out of this powerful addiction of the mind. Today my mind is being restored back to a normal way of thinking and I am living life again and am enjoying life without gambling.

The worldwide gambling industry has flourished and is growing at a rapid rate with the money that they collect from gambling losers and not gambling winners. These casinos worldwide take in millions of dollars daily. The worldwide gambling industry is on the increase and so is the number of addicted compulsive or pathological gamblers. Gambling addiction is a disease and has reached worldwide epidemic proportions.

The gambling industry is a very huge money making game created to take the hard earned money from addicted gambling fools. The gambling games are fixed and are designed or programmed in favor of the casino or other gambling business. Casino bosses are aware that the general public are like sheep and can be easily brainwashed and fooled.

The various entertaining interactive slot machines are computer generated and are run by a main computer within the casino. Casino computer wizards can see which slot machines are paying out money and need to be adjusted so that the casino takes in money instead of disbursing money to gamblers. Technicians do adjust the slot machines and this is usually performed in the middle of the night when the casino floor is somewhat empty. It is very hard to win against a sophisticated programmed high tech computer.

Dealing cards is a very simple task unless your job as a dealer is to take in money for your casino employer. In order to accomplish this goal the card dealers have to attend a dealer's school for several weeks. In the card dealing schools the students are taught how to manipulate a card deck so that the casino wins the majority of the games and takes in money. Counting cards is a skill for advanced dealers in the gambling industry. It is illegal for gamblers to count cards but is okay if the card dealers count cards.

The sexy well-endowed cocktail waitresses are a big attraction for gambling addicts. The job of the cocktail waitress is to alter the brain chemistry of gamblers by feeding them free alcohol. The gambler's mental perception also will change and they will lose sense of reality and enter into a gambling fantasy with the more alcohol that they place into their bloodstream. These sexy cocktail waitresses also have the need for greed because as part of the casino industry game they take in a lot of money from tips from the addicted compulsive or pathological gambler.

Gambling can be a lot of fun until it becomes an insidious mental addiction. Gambling is probably the hardest addiction to stop because it is a behavioral and mental addiction of the mind. The leaders in the gambling industry know that gambling is a strong addiction of the mind and that it is possible to control gambler's minds. Once a gambler's mind is controlled by gambling then their finances can also be controlled.

The gambling industry is growing and will con-tinue to grow and has become a major player in the political and economics of the United States and other countries worldwide. The major goal and character and goal of a capitalist society is the need for greed.

CONCLUSION

Gambling is everywhere and has become socially acceptable as normal behavior. Gambling is abnormal behavior that appears to be normal behavior for the addicted compulsive or pathological gambler who is consumed with this powerful addiction of the mind disease. There are millions of addicted gamblers within the United States as well as worldwide and gambling addiction has become a serious disease epidemic.

Medical professionals have agreed after several studies that gambling addiction is a psychiatric disorder and a disease. The disease is centered in the brain and can be genetically predisposed. The same part of the brain that is affected by alcohol or drug addiction is the same place that is affected by gambling addiction. Addicted gamblers can get a mental high while exercising their addiction. Being addicted to video poker is compared to being addicted to crack cocaine.

Gambling addiction is a very powerful addiction. This ugly addiction of the mind takes over a person's whole being that includes their cognitive processes, emotions, and spirit. Addiction to gambling can also be combined with other addictions like alcohol, drugs, smoking, or sex.

Gambling appeals to the fantasy side of one's thought processes. A person does not wake up from their gambling addiction until they hit an emotional bottom and experience a rude awakening and start to emerge out of their fantasy world and into the real world. Financial debt can be a reality check or trigger that helps many addicted gamblers snap out of their addiction. Many times this happens when their car gets repossessed or their home goes through a foreclosure or they have to file for bankruptcy. Sometimes their family will leave them and a separation or a divorce will also cause a gambler to come to terms with their gambling addiction.

Many gambling addicts want to escape reality so they choose to remain in the fantasy world of gambling. They become a fantasy gambler who is lost in self-delusion and denial. Constant living in a fantasy world can be crazy making. This fantasy world also causes gamblers to be very secretive about their gambling addiction. We are certainly as sick as our secrets.

Living in this fantasy world and not living in reality causes compulsive or pathological gamblers to get themselves in major financial debt. This debt can be mostly credit cards, personal loans, or payday loans. An addicted gambler loses all sense of financial responsibility when it comes to maintaining a sound healthy financial budget. Gambling causes wreck less spending and borrowing. They do not think clearly due to the cognitive distortion that is caused by the gambling addiction.

Many medical emergencies happen to sick addicted gamblers as a direct result of their addiction. These medical emergencies are kept hushed and the doctors will never mention gambling as a cause for the medical condition. Even when a gambler commits suicide the doctors will never mention gambling as the cause. Hospitals in Las Vegas receive about 30 patients per day into their emergency room as a direct result of gambling addiction.

A drunk and distraught gambler could leave a casino or gambling bar after losing hundreds of dollars and get into a car accident injuring himself or other innocent people. A sick gambler could also go home and assault their family members or sometimes beat up a complete stranger. Many gambling addicts will also experience anxiety attacks or heart attacks. As a result of depression and severe gambler's remorse, many sick gamblers will kill themself as they perceive death as the only way out of the misery of their gambling addiction.

There are several incidents where gamblers in Las Vegas have committed suicide by jumping off of a casino balcony or from the top of a parking garage. Some will walk across a major freeway so that a fast moving automobile will hit them. Others have killed themselves in their hotel room. These suicides caused by gambling addiction are kept hushed by casino management and local law enforcement and do not make it into the news media.

Gambling is growing at an alarming rate and gambling environments are everywhere. This is why we have millions of compulsive or pathological gamblers worldwide. Gambling environments are also very addicting along side with the gambling games. The fantasy gambling environments provide an atmosphere for gambling addiction to be nurtured. A person who does not want to deal with real life problems can easily escape into a casino or gambling bar and into the fantasy world of gambling.

Americans can wager legally in almost 1,000 casinos in the United States. About 500 Las Vegas style casinos operate in 11 states and about 500 casinos are on American Indian reservations in 29 states. In addition, 11 states are exploring laws that would allow the existing race tracks to convert into what would be called racinos. There is also the internet computer gambling that can also be very addicting because many people are already addicted to the internet.

Many corporations and politicians are becoming very wealthy at the expense of the sick addicted gambler. This disease and addiction of the mind has been kept hushed for too long by the gambling industry, our governments, and the news media. This hidden epidemic of gambling addiction has to be exposed before more lives are destroyed.

My hope is that this book has shed some light about the dark side of gambling addiction. The goal in writing this book is that many people worldwide will understand more about gambling addiction and that many active addicted gamblers will come to terms with their gambling addiction and get into recovery.

My biggest realization after coming out on my gambling addiction is that I do not have to gamble to enjoy life and that it is okay not to gamble. There is more to life than throwing away your hard earned money into a gambling machine or a table game in order to get a free drink.